the
DEATH
of PRIDE

*Learning to
Stand from a
Fallen King*

PAUL VANDERVEER

**NEXT
RESOURCE**

*For Mallory, Haddie, Eden, Micaiah, Elisha, Ari,
and all the family at Lakewood Christian Church who
have so often given their unconditional love and the
encouragement to dream big for the kingdom.*

*Also, for Virginia, you would have loved this and
been one of the earliest and greatest supporters.*

Contents

How to Use This Resource

This resource is meant as a tool for you to use in your life. However, the best tool is worthless if you don't know how to use it. What follows is a suggestion on how to best use this tool. It is by no means the only way this tool can or should be used, but merely an explanation of how this resource has been designed to be of the most benefit to you.

This resource is not meant to be a passive exercise. Our hope is that you will engage with this material as you study it. At the conclusion of each chapter, you will be encouraged to engage with what you have read, to work through the issues raised in the text as well as your own experiences, and to take the next step when you finish by using what you have studied and learned as a springboard into deeper study and application.

We want to emphasize that this resource is best experienced in community with others. Whether as a part of a small group or with a friend, we encourage you to see and approach this book as a shared journey of transformation.

Each chapter will explore different elements surrounding a topic or scripture. At the end of each chapter, we'll ask five questions:

What have you learned from this? Was there something you hadn't thought of before? Was there an idea you knew, but that hit differently as you read? How were you challenged? What are your struggles in this area of focus?

What can you do with this? Moments of conviction, while being good, are only beneficial if we apply them and move from them.

What are a few specific ways you can apply the truths of this portion to your life?

How can you pray through this? Talk with God about these things. You can write a prayer, or simply put everything down for a moment and talk with God about how He can use the things you've read or learned to continue transforming you.

Who do you need to talk to about this? Who do you know that would benefit from the things you've read? Who is going through this study with you? Do you disagree with or not understand something? This section is a place to think through anyone you feel moved to talk to as you learn.

What can this look like in the church? While personal growth is an important and major goal of this resource, as a church we are called to grow together. How can the things you are learning be applied to your local faith family? How can you be a part of bringing this larger growth to life?

What's Next? At the end of the day, Scripture is the ultimate authority. With that in mind, this section will give a list of pertinent verses in Scripture that deal with the topics at hand. While the list may not be exhaustive, it is a good start in personal study which can serve as a springboard from which you can seek the whole counsel of God in the deep well of Scripture.

Further Resources: This book is certainly not the last word on this topic. I stand on the shoulders of many who have come before me. At the end of this book, there will be a section where I list every book, sermon, or article that informed this study, as well as other works which can offer further understanding and different perspectives.

Preface

When I was ten years old, I had one goal in life: mow the lawn. To be in control of a machine with blades that spun at terrifying speeds and calmly walk behind it felt very manly to me, and I so wanted to do manly things. Also, my grandfather had announced that he would pay twenty dollars for the work. For a ten-year-old, that was a small fortune so I was more than a little enthusiastic about the opportunity. I quickly volunteered for the job, only to be told by my father that ten was too young an age to mow the lawn and that I would have to wait until I turned thirteen. Over the next two summers, I enviously watched as my older brothers mowed the lawn and counted their money—sometimes right in front of me. The summer I turned thirteen, my grandfather said to me, "Well, I guess it's about time you came over and mowed my yard." These were the words I had not-so-patiently waited for. That night, before bed, I laid out my clothes in preparation: old shoes, long pants, light-colored t-shirt, Space Jam hat, and the coolest pair of sunglasses I could find. I was ready.

The next morning, I woke early, dressed, and made my way across the street to where my grandfather was already standing in his driveway, mower by his side. As I walked up, he said, "Okay, I'm going to take you through how all this works and then get you started." Unbeknownst to my grandfather, over the last two summers I had dedicated myself to the study of lawn mowing. I thought I should humbly and subtly inform him of my profound expertise. "Grandpa," I began, "I don't need any help. I know what I'm doing."

Subtlety was something I had yet to study. My grandfather raised his eyebrows and told me, "By all means, have at it." I pulled my cap down firmly on my head as I approached the mower. I pushed in the primer and then lifted the arm into the operating position. I had arrived at the moment of truth. Reaching down, I grabbed the pull cord and gave it the strongest pull my thirteen-year-old arm could manage. The sudden sound of the mower roaring to life was the sound of success to me. Glancing over to my grandfather, I gave a self-satisfied expression that said, "I told you I could do it," to which he nodded and said, "Very impressive." As he took his position in a chair on the porch with a glass of iced tea, I got to work.

Until that moment, I had failed to realize that there was a difference between watching someone mow the lawn and the actual experience of mowing a lawn. As I began to push the mower across the yard, I was struck by how difficult it was. My brothers had made it seem effortless, but pushing the thing back and forth took about every ounce of strength I had. Over the next two hours, I struggled to push the lawn mower back and forth across the grass, all while my grandfather sat on the porch sipping his iced tea. Finally finished, I collapsed on the driveway gasping for breath. As I lay there creating my own little sweat angel on the pavement, my grandfather walked over. Still sipping his tea, he said as he pointed, "You know, if you were to pull that lever right there, the mower would have moved itself and then you could have just walked behind it." Before I could fully comprehend the meaning of his words, he took another sip and said, "Make sure you put it back in the garage when you're done here," before going inside where I am certain he had a good laugh.

There have been many moments in my life when a little bit of humility could have saved me a lot of heartache. Unfortunately for me, this was not the summer I overcame pride. In fact, this was the most painless story I could think to share. Battling pride has consumed far more of my life than I ever thought it would. When I look back over the years, I see so many times where my thoughts and actions tempt me to hang my head in shame of what my pride has stolen from me. However, I do not believe I'm alone in this, which is both a comfort and a concern. It's comforting to have solidarity with others; however, this same commonality is more of a concern and here's why. Sins that are experienced by most are far too often diminished to the point of being acceptable, so long as they are held in check. We become okay with pride because it is a burden shared by many, if not most of us. However, pride, as we will discover in the following pages, is the root cause of not only our greatest struggles but of the worst atrocities and greatest miseries of our world. It is a poison that eats away and kills the soul from the inside out and must be addressed if we are ever to experience the joyous and purposeful life God has created for us. The good news, however, is that there is a cure.

In this book we will endeavor to identify pride at its source, using as our case study the Old Testament king of Babylon, Nebuchadnezzar. In the first part of this book, Chapters 1-5, we will discuss the magnificent fall of the great king Nebuchadnezzar, gleaning from his story insights to aid us in overcoming pride. Then in the second part, we will take the insights we have learned from Nebuchadnezzar and step from them into a gospel-centered journey with Jesus. This journey will cost more yet yield a greater return than you can fathom, but at its end you will cross the threshold into the kingdom of heaven having been transformed into the likeness of Christ who greets you as a friend.

Like everything in the Christian life, we are not meant to walk these paths alone. We encourage you to commit not only to taking this journey but to doing it with a trusted friend or small group. The QR code to the right will connect you to our online resources, including further study materials, video courses, one-on-one counseling, and group discussion questions. We look forward to taking this journey with you.

My prayers are for you as you begin this path. May you be blessed in its undertaking.

Acknowledgments

I t feels odd that my name appears as the author of this book when it was brought to life by the encouragement, feedback, stories, and insight freely offered by so many. I would, however, like to make special mention of a few who directly inspired and aided in this writing.

My wife, Mallory, has been a source of joy and encouragement that is far beyond what I deserve.

My children, for making me a father, and thinking that this book is "really cool." My prayer is that you will be my greatest contribution to the kingdom of heaven.

My first editor, Scott Walker, read every word of this book, even when the chapters were an embarrassing cacophony of random thoughts with no discernable path. You gave your honest and sometimes brutal feedback openly because you believed that this resource matters. Thank you for shining light on the path.

The team of readers, Dan, Pat, Rick, Keith, Paul, Larry, Jim, Ann Marie, Ken, Mom, Dad, and Mallory. You were honest and right. Thank you.

My grandfather, Gaither, who instilled in me at a young age to follow God even and especially when I don't feel equipped for the journey. Thank you for your legacy and guidance.

My father, Greg, has shown me the power that comes from redeemed stories. Thank you for showing me what a man of God is.

My mother, Paula, for the many times you have prayed over me. Thank you for showing me so often that we serve a big God who can do the unimaginable.

My friend, Michael Rogers, who guided me through some of the pitfalls of writing.

The elders of Lakewood Christian Church, for their enduring encouragement and allowing the space for big kingdom visions.

The family at Lakewood Christian Church, for loving me and my family unconditionally.

Roy, thank you for telling a stranger to let go to get God. Our meeting was a divine appointment, one I will never forget or fail to be thankful for.

Larry, Paul, and Jim, Lakewood may never know how much they have been blessed by your wisdom, prayers, and insight given at our Friday morning small group, but I do and I'm grateful. Thank you.

This list could go on far longer to include every mentor and friend who has shaped my faith journey. I remember you often and thank you for all of it, especially the hard parts.

This book is a small addition to a very large collection of those who have endeavored to place the kingdom in front of people through the written word. I stand on many shoulders that are stronger than mine. I am grateful. Sincerely, thank you all.

Introduction

It hadn't exactly been the easiest of monarchies, but, overall, Nebuchadnezzar felt that his time as ruler had been a successful endeavor. During his reign, Babylon had conquered kingdoms, taken slaves, and grown the empire into one that was admired and feared across the world. He hadn't met an enemy he could not vanquish, yet there were a few formidable adversaries that still gave his heart pause when he recounted them. It wouldn't be fair to call the God of Daniel an adversary, though they had found themselves on opposite sides in the past. However, in every encounter, Nebuchadnezzar had witnessed a power that left him puzzled even now.

After the defeat of Israel, Nebuchadnezzar had been told of Daniel's and his friends' dedication to the practices of their religion. It was the policy of Babylon not to allow any hint of rebellion in those who were being assimilated into the Babylonian culture, so Nebuchadnezzar had first intended to react harshly toward this. However, when the report came that their physical health and physique far out measured the others in the program, Nebuchadnezzar decided it was an acceptable allowance. He thought the best empire in the world should have the best captives in the world, and Daniel and his friends were perfect examples. At the time, Nebuchadnezzar hadn't attributed any of it to the power of the God of the Israelites, he simply assumed the four captives were putting in extra effort to maintain their exceptional physique.

As Nebuchadnezzar walked on his roof, he chuckled to himself, amazed at how seemingly independent things connect when looking at them in hindsight. He remembered the dream that had plagued him not long after hearing about Daniel. He remembered the distrust and fury at his own so-called "wise men" who were not able to reveal the dream or its meaning—to the point that he had concluded all his advisors were swindlers worthy of death. But then, there was Daniel . . . again. He had come before Nebuchadnezzar and had not only revealed the dream but gave it a meaning that could only be true. He recounted with great joy how his Babylon was depicted as the golden head atop a statue of lesser kingdoms. He was slightly disheartened to think of the future degradation of what he had spent his life building, but to know that he was the king at the pinnacle of a kingdom was an overwhelming source of pride for him.

He then recounted the building of his statue as a wonder to be beheld. Standing ninety feet tall and shining in gold, it was an impressive sight that lauded the glory of Babylon. Naturally, Nebuchadnezzar had assumed all would want to pay homage to this symbol of Babylon's success, but as its dedication came nearer, a concern grew within him. *What if not all the people of the kingdom would bow?* Few knew how fragile empires could be. Great fires are started with a single spark, and it was possible that one hint of rebellion could begin something that would eventually bring about the destruction of his life's work. One of the talents Nebuchadnezzar had cultivated in his time was the ability to see problems from far away. In fact, he attributed most of his success to this skill. So how would he cut off this potential fire of rebellion? With a fire of his own.

Certainly, the fear of burning alive would be enough to quell the reluctance of even the most ardent of anarchists, but even if it wasn't, swift justice awaited that would trumpet the resolve of the king. As the day approached, Nebuchadnezzar had a furnace placed in view of his grand statue. It was a bit of an eyesore, but the point it made was unmistakable.

The decree went out:

> You are commanded, O peoples, nations, and languages, that when you hear the sound of the horn, pipe, lyre, trigon, harp, bagpipe, and every kind of music, you are to fall down and

worship the golden image that King Nebuchadnezzar has set up. And whoever does not fall down and worship shall immediately be cast into a burning fiery furnace. (Dan. 3:4–6)

The king waited with gleeful anticipation to see all of the peoples of Babylon united in worship of the nation. At his signal the instruments rang out with such a sound that the ground vibrated and all fell to their faces before mighty Babylon.

At least, that was the plan.

After the call to worship, some of the king's advisers came into his presence and told him of three Hebrew captives, Shadrach, Meshach, and Abednego, who had failed to bow before his statue. These men were known to the king. They were counterparts of the interpreter, Daniel, and had been put in positions of authority themselves. Nebuchadnezzar still hadn't come to a place of completely trusting his advisers, but he was enraged that anyone would so blatantly stand against his decree. So he had the three men brought before him. While he was no stranger to violence, he had made a point to use force only when it expedited his own agenda. In this case, he was prepared to follow through on his threat, but he wanted to be certain of their disobedience before carrying out the sentence.

As the Hebrew men came before him, he wasted no time. "Is it true," the king asked, "O Shadrach, Meshach, and Abednego, that you do not serve my gods or worship the golden image that I have set up? Now if you are ready when you hear the sound of the horn, pipe, lyre, trigon, harp, bagpipe, and every kind of music, to fall down and worship the image that I have made, well and good. But if you do not worship, you shall immediately be cast into a burning fiery furnace. And who is the god who will deliver you out of my hands?" (Dan. 3:14–15). Nebuchadnezzar had been particularly proud of that last part. He knew these Hebrews worshipped a God to which they ascribed significant powers, but they needed to learn the difference between an abstract God and the reality of fire presently awaiting them should they, once again, fail to comply.

If the king was angered at their initial refusal, his anger was turned to unbridled rage at their next response: "O Nebuchadnezzar," they said, "we have no need to answer you in this matter. If this be so, our God whom we serve is able to deliver us from the burning fiery furnace, and he will deliver us out of your hand, O king. But if not, be it known to you, O king, that we will not serve your gods or worship the golden image that you have set up" (Dan. 3:16–18). The king was beside himself. *We have no need to answer you in this matter?* He was the king of the greatest empire on earth. The audacity of these mere children was enough to be admired had it not been directed at him. Not only had they refused to give an answer for their behavior, but they had also claimed no fear of anything he could do to them. This was an outrageous affront. How dare they mock Babylon? How dare they turn their noses to the certain death the king had promised? In his anger Nebuchadnezzar ordered that the fires be stoked to such an intensity that it mirrored his own rage. Once he was satisfied with the fire's fury, he had the men bound and thrown into its flames by some of his best warriors.

What happened next still perplexed Nebuchadnezzar. He saw the men thrown into the fire, he watched as his warriors were overcome by the flames, he looked at their bodies now lying dead before the furnace, but he didn't hear the screams he had been expecting. Had the fire been so hot that they were overcome before they were able to feel the pain of it? But as the king lifted his eyes to the flames, he saw something that contradicted reason. In the midst of the fire, he saw the shadows of not three, but four men. They were not writhing, nor begging, they were simply walking around. This would have been enough for the king to challenge his own sanity, but when he looked at the fourth figure in the fire, he noticed that it shone with a light that could only be described as angelic.

The king looked up at the stars as he remembered these things. The pinpricks of light in the inky black sky reminded him of the light that shone from the angelic being and how from that moment, beside a fiery furnace, he had decided that the God of the Hebrews was not a God with which one would want to trifle. In an effort to placate the God of Shadrach, Meshach, and Abednego, the king had instituted a decree that the worship of their God would not only be accepted in the kingdom but protected throughout all the empire. Not only that, but he had also promoted the three young Hebrews to positions of greater power and responsibility. It was fair to say that the king believed he had learned his lesson when it came to the dealings with this living God of theirs. The years since had been fruitful. The kingdom had flourished, and the majesty of Babylon had grown to even greater heights than it had previously seen, but then the dreams returned.

Only a little more than a year ago, the king remembered, he had been lying in his bed in his palace, enjoying the diversions and amenities that came with his station, when he was overtaken by a dream that greatly alarmed him. He often dreamed of one thing or another, but this dream held with it the same weight as his dream from many years before. He awoke and, at once, knew that even if he could not understand its meaning, its implications were certain. He had called his advisers in and was once again disappointed by their limitations.

Finally, Daniel walked into the chamber and Nebuchadnezzar shared his dream with all the detail he could recall: "The visions of my head as I lay in bed were these," said Nebuchadnezzar, "I saw, and behold, a tree in the midst of the earth, and its height was great. The tree grew and became strong, and its top reached to heaven, and it was visible to the end of the whole earth. Its leaves were beautiful and its fruit abundant, and in it was food for all. The beasts of the field found shade under it, and the birds of the heavens lived in its branches, and all flesh was fed from it. I saw in the visions of my head as I lay in bed, and behold, a watcher, a holy one, came down from heaven. He proclaimed aloud and said thus: 'Chop down the tree and lop off its branches, strip off its leaves and scatter its fruit. Let the beasts flee from under it and the birds from its branches. But leave the stump of its roots in the earth, bound with a band of iron and bronze, amid the tender grass of the field.'"

The king now spoke with more urgency as sweat began to collect on his brow, "'Let him be wet with the dew of heaven. Let his portion be with the beasts in the grass of the earth. Let his mind be changed from a man's, and let a beast's mind be given to him; and let seven periods of time pass over him. The sentence is by the decree of the watchers, the decision by the word of the holy ones, to the end that the living may know that the Most High rules the kingdom of men and gives it to whom he will and sets over it the lowliest of men.'" The king let out a heavy sigh, placed his arms at his sides, and said, "This dream I, King Nebuchadnezzar, saw. And you, O Belteshazzar (Daniel), tell me the interpretation, because all the wise men of my kingdom are not able to make known to me the interpretation, but you are able, for the spirit of the holy gods is in you" (Dan. 4:10–18).

Daniel's eyes spoke long before his voice found words. As the king watched, Daniel's face changed from listening, to alarm, and finally rested on sorrow. When he spoke, it was with a heavy voice. "My Lord," he said, "may the dream be for those who hate you and its interpretation for your enemies" (Dan. 4:19). Daniel went on to tell the king the tree he envisioned did not represent Babylon as the statue had from his previous dream, but that it represented Nebuchadnezzar himself. With this revelation, the rest of the dream's meaning fell into place. The king would be chopped down, he would be driven from his palace and wealth to make his home in the fields with the livestock, and he would remain that way until he knew that God was the ruler over the kingdoms of men.

Nebuchadnezzar didn't react to this news in perhaps the way he would have in his earlier years. He didn't respond with fury, he didn't make a decree, he simply looked at Daniel and asked a question in a tone that was almost a plea, "Can anything be done?" Daniel responded, "Let my counsel be acceptable to you: break off your sins by practicing righteousness, and your iniquities by showing mercy to the oppressed, that there may perhaps be a lengthening of your prosperity" (Dan. 4:27). The king steeled himself and made a vow in his heart that he would do all that Daniel had suggested. He would become a benevolent king who, in all his ways, acknowledged God alone as the ruler of Babylon and all the kingdoms of the world. He would make it his mission to live in humility and servitude. It wasn't that the king was exactly happy with this arrangement, but, when faced with the alternative, he jumped at the chance to placate a God whom he knew to have great power and authority. This went on quite successfully for the next year, which brings us once again to the king, walking alone on the rooftop of the palace, pondering his kingdom.

It was one of those perfect nights with only enough humidity to carry the scent of flowers through the air in such a way that every breath was filled with the sweetness of their nectar. As the king strode along looking to the farthest reaches of his eyesight at his kingdom, he was struck by its beauty and strength. He looked at the lights that flickered in the homes beneath him, knowing that his reign had provided not only the fuel for those flames but also the security that the families felt in their dwellings. His eyes shifted to the barracks, knowing that they housed only a fraction of the armies that would be available should he but speak a command. Breathing in the night air, taking in his kingdom, he let out a breath and spoke, "Is not this great Babylon, which I have built by my mighty power as a royal residence and for the glory of my majesty?" (Dan. 4:30).

Before the words were finished leaving his mouth, the sky opened and a voice spoke, not in shouts, but with such volume that Nebuchadnezzar could hardly breathe from the vibration. It said, "O king Nebuchadnezzar, to you it is spoken: The kingdom has departed from you." (Dan. 4:31). The king felt a fear he had never experienced before. Fear of such strength that he believed he would die from it, but it lasted only for a moment, for in the next moment his mind left him, and he knew no more.

PART ONE

The King

1

Defining Pride

In preparation for this book, I had conversations with several people in which I asked the question, "What is pride?" I received answers circling around the notions of conceit, narcissism, an inability to be wrong, and other similar sentiments. While most people would agree that each of those words constitutes a prideful attitude, I believe that conceit, narcissism, and an inability to be wrong are simply symptoms of a more foundational struggle.

I have a dear friend who recently found himself writhing in pain on the floor of his living room. His stomach was distended, and he began vomiting bile as he called for an ambulance. Once at the hospital, they gave him pain medications and inserted a tube into his stomach to drain the fluid that had gathered there. What was initially thought to be appendicitis was then diagnosed as a blockage in his small intestinal tract, causing his bowel to become dormant. Over the following two weeks, he remained in the hospital until there was proof of movement once more in the cavernous depths of his bowel. I have had many unique experiences as a pastor and sitting in a hospital room celebrating with a family over the bowel movement of a sixty-year-old man tops the list.

After two weeks in the hospital, my friend was finally released to go home. We celebrated, but our celebrations did not last long. Only days after his return home, he was rushed to a hospital by ambulance. By the time I arrived, he had already gone through surgery. When I walked into his room in the ICU, I was shocked at what I saw. My friend, who before was a strong and powerful guy, looked small. He lay on a bed with three drains coming out of different parts of his abdomen. He had been placed on a ventilator and kept in a semi-conscious state. By the end of the whole ordeal, he stayed in the hospital for a little over two months. During that time and for another month after, he was not able to eat solid foods.

It turned out that a clot had formed in his small intestine. However, the intestine was not dormant like they had thought. Three feet of his small intestine had died and begun to decompose inside him. After having three feet of his intestines removed, he was able to begin the slow process of healing. While the healing took longer than he wanted, it was still a relief for him to know that he was, in fact, healing. The reason I share this story is that my friend's healing would never have been possible if they had only treated him symptomatically. The doctors could have addressed the fluid buildup to cure his pain and left it at that. But something was dead inside him. So before he could truly heal, it had to be removed. For us, in thinking about pride and how it affects our lives, we must look past the outward signs of pride—its symptoms—and discern how it is rooted in our hearts, because we're not simply looking to treat the painful symptoms of pride. We need a cure.

Pride is one of those words that most can acknowledge, but few can define. We know the symptoms of pride and can probably tell a few stories where pride played a destructive role, some of which feature ourselves as the antagonists. Still, the question remains: what is pride at its core? Looking at Nebuchadnezzar's fall offers poignant insight into the dangers of hidden pride.

In the grand palaces of Babylon, King Nebuchadnezzar ruled with absolute authority. His kingdom stretched far and wide—its influence unmatched and its splendor undeniable. The city was adorned with magnificent architecture; its walls were a testament to the strength and ingenuity of its people. The Hanging Gardens, one of the wonders of the ancient world, stood as a symbol of Nebuchadnezzar's power and the wealth of his empire. To many, the king was god-like, the very epitome of success, wisdom, and might. So what caused Nebuchadnezzar's downfall? You guessed it. Pride.

Standing on his rooftop, looking out at the wonders of his kingdom, Nebuchadnezzar said, "I have built this great kingdom for the glory of my majesty." This declaration seems to have been the end of God's patience with him. I want you to notice, though, that what brought about his humiliation was not only the words Nebuchadnezzar spoke but the attitude of his heart. Your mouth will eventually speak the truths your heart believes. In that moment on his rooftop, Nebuchadnezzar spoke from his heart, believing he was the one who deserved the glory for the kingdom of Babylon.

God is the only one who deserves glory, honor, and praise. Daniel says: "Blessed be the name of God forever and ever, to whom belong wisdom and might. He changes times and seasons; he removes kings and sets up kings; he gives wisdom to the wise and knowledge to those who have understanding" (Dan. 2:20–21). Nebuchadnezzar's sin was not reveling in his position of power; his sin was in the belief that he alone was sovereign, that the kingdom he reigned over existed for his own glory. Nebuchadnezzar had already been shown—several showstopping times—that the God of the Hebrews was a living God, with sovereignty over dreams and nature. Nebuchadnezzar had witnessed these things, yet there was still a belief deep within him that the fortune of his kingdom was in his hands for his own glory. In that moment, the true belief of his heart rose to the surface, and he claimed credit for a glory that solely belonged to God.

Throughout the Hebrew Old Testament, pride is most often referred to with the noun *gā'ôn*, which, when translated to English, is the word for "height."[1] So when the Bible talks of pride, it's essentially saying we are making ourselves higher than we ought. We're thinking too highly of ourselves or elevating our importance and significance past the point where God has placed us. However, when we look further into the Hebrew use of the word *gā'ôn*, there is another meaning. While being used to describe pride, this word also describes the majesty and height of God. It's not coincidental that this one word describes two seemingly divergent ideas. Both give an understanding of something far above our grasp, but for God, the word rightly describes the level at which He alone resides. This understanding of height completely and appropriately conveys His sovereignty, while, in comparison, makes us more like little children reaching for something we were never meant to have.

As far as a working definition of pride, I suggest that it is when we elevate ourselves to a position that rightfully belongs to God.

Pride is when we elevate our desires to the same importance as God's.

When we take our own desires, plans, and understanding and elevate them to the same weight and importance as those of God, that is pride working in us. We can see this not just in the case of Nebuchadnezzar but throughout Scripture, even from the very beginning. In Genesis 3, God had created the world and everything in it and called it good. Within His creation, in a garden that provided for their every need, stood Adam and Eve. God gave them the freedom to do anything that seemed good to them with only one exception: don't eat the fruit from one tree. Like children, we don't always respond well when we are told not to do something.

When I was about five years old, any time my mother made pie, she would allow me to sit on the counter and "help" her. One time, we had only just started to place the dough in a pie dish when the phone rang. My mother took off her apron and walked toward the door. To this day, I stand behind my belief that had she simply walked out of the room without saying anything, what followed would not have been so tragic and scarring, literally. But as my mother walked out of the room, she turned and said to that sweet five-year-old boy, "I'm going to answer the phone, and while I'm gone, don't put your hand in the toaster."

To this day, I blame my mother for what happened next. We were making a pie. At no point was the toaster a part of this process, nor was it even mentioned in conversation. The toaster sat innocently against the wall. However, her brief and reckless mention of it as she left the room, I believe, set the stage for the tragic events that followed. Having heard her word of caution, my five-year-old brain started to wander from the path of righteousness. Questions, one after another, ran through my mind. *Why would I put my hand in the toaster? Why wouldn't she want me to put my hand in the toaster? What's in the toaster? Is she hiding something in the toaster?*

These questions then gave way to assertions. *I bet there's candy in the toaster! She's very selfish for hoarding all the candy to herself. I should check out this toaster. It's too dark, I should verify that there is in fact candy in the toaster. I should put my hand in the toaster.*

And not long after, the pitiful screams of a disobedient five-year-old filled the house.

While my thoughts from back then are likely slightly exaggerated, it is a similar progression that we can see in how we as humans respond to the authority of God. In Genesis 3, God gave Adam and Eve one command: don't eat from this one tree. So what did Adam and Eve do? Much like the young child who scooted over to the toaster, they were close to the tree, and Satan was ready to pounce. How did he do it exactly? Five-year-old me, about a day after the toaster incident, would have recognized the line of questioning:

> Now the serpent was more crafty than any other beast of the field that the LORD God had made. He said to the woman, "Did God actually say, 'You shall not eat of any tree in the garden'?" And the woman said to the serpent, "We may eat of the fruit of the trees in the garden, but God said, 'You shall not eat of the fruit of the tree that is in the midst of the garden, neither shall you touch it, lest you die.'" But the serpent said to the woman, "You will not surely die. For God knows that when you eat of it your eyes will be opened, and you will be like God, knowing good and evil" (Gen. 3:1–5).

The interesting thing about this passage is the tactic Satan used in getting Eve to break her covenant with God. First, he called into question the validity of God's warning. "Did he seriously say you can't eat fruit?" This simple question implies an accusation of God being unreasonable in His commands. Eve's response, then, is one of defense for God. "No, he said we could eat anything. We're just not allowed to eat the fruit off of this one tree, lest we die." Satan had brought her directly to this point, and in Genesis 3:5, he drove his temptation home: "You will not surely die. For God knows that when you eat of it your eyes will be opened, and you will be like God, knowing good and evil." What a crafty serpent indeed. He began his questioning with an implied accusation. He then finished with a direct reproach of God's character by painting Him as a withholder of good and desirable things. Who wouldn't want to be like God? This desire seems to have good intentions behind it. If we had more knowledge and understanding, we could do so much more for God. The temptation that compromised Eve's devotion was the desire to be like God, to step into His position and hold His knowledge. If the definition of pride is placing yourself in a position that rightfully belongs to God, then the first sin was one of pride. Therefore, Adam and Eve, seeking God's ultimate knowledge and sovereignty, placed themselves in a position beyond their own ability and far from their created purpose.

Psalm 139:6 says, "Such knowledge is too wonderful for me; it is high; I cannot attain it." We do not have the ability to contain nor survive the complete knowledge of God. I once heard a pastor give this illustration: Imagine that every ocean, lake, river, stream, swimming pool, puddle, and every drop of water in the world represents the understanding and knowledge of God. Now imagine that your understanding is every drop of water that can fit into a six-ounce coffee cup. To say that something can't be, simply because we can't understand it, is to say that every ocean, lake, river, stream, swimming pool, and puddle can't exist because they don't fit into our coffee cup.

The knowledge of God is so far above us, and the tendency of pride is to place ourselves in the position of ultimate authority in our lives. So, in a seemingly elevated position, we lack the knowledge and wisdom to sustain us. From our perceived place of power, we make decisions concerning our pursuits and desires that ultimately prove disastrous. We strive after the very things that would destroy us. We crave autonomy and control, which can cause us to carve out our own plans and destiny, resulting in a life of many great merits and wonderful accomplishments—but without God, which of our accomplishments can hold lasting, eternal value?

We must come to see pride for what it is: a poison that kills from the inside out, eating its way through our souls and leaving us as a shell of unrealized potential for the kingdom of God. Pride robs us of our true purpose. This is why Scripture so ardently speaks against it. Pride blinds us and tricks us into giving great value to temporary things, all while relegating eternal things to a status of being potentially important but practically insignificant.

The craftiness of pride, however, is that many would agree with its definition without ascribing it to themselves. Pride is a sin that is easily seen in the lives of others yet remains mysteriously hidden from our own awareness. Scripture teaches that pride is the source of all sin. C. S. Lewis in his seminal work on the Christian life, *Mere Christianity*, said, "Unchastity, greed, anger, drunkenness, and all that, are mere fleabites in comparison: it was through pride that the devil became the devil: Pride leads to every other vice: it is the complete anti-God state of mind."[2] Later in the chapter, Lewis says, "Pride, which has been the chief cause of misery in every nation and every family since the world began . . ."[3] If you were to look at your struggles beyond your actions to the heart, you would find pride at its root. We would never believe we are intentionally elevating ourselves to that of the position of God. Still, when we look at what we value in life, how our decisions are made, or where we place our security, it doesn't take long to see the tendrils of pride squeezing our hearts.

In seemingly small ways, pride often plays a part in the way we make decisions. Going even deeper, the posture of our heart in the way we make decisions says a lot about where our trust rests and who, ultimately, is leading our life. Not too long ago, my wife, Mallory, and I were deciding whether to buy a camper. We had saved and talked about it for years, knowing it could be a good investment for time with our children while they were still in the house. I had done a fair amount of research and was more than ready to make the jump. My wife, who sometimes struggles in the face of making a final decision, suddenly decided we needed to pray about our motives and whether it truly would be good for our family. In my heavenly wisdom, I responded with something close to: "Mallory, I think God is okay with it; let's just buy the stinkin' camper." Truthfully, I hadn't uttered a single prayer on the subject. I possibly reasoned that the matter was far too small of an issue to involve the Almighty. Though, most likely, I wasn't interested in any outside influence that might speak against my desires.

A camper is a small thing. I don't think we tilted the balance of heaven or hell with our purchase, but my heart posture in the face of that decision is troubling to me. It's not that I didn't need the input of God; it's that I didn't want His voice or His leading in that moment. What haunts me is this: how many other areas of my life do I shut out holy input under the guise of feeling like I don't need help or guidance? In our lives, we face many decisions, like who we marry, how many kids we'd like to have, our job, what we save for, which school our children attend, which sports they play, and many others. Very often, we make these decisions based solely on our own priorities, what *we* think is right.

What we value dictates our priorities. As we go through life making decisions, too often seeking the wisdom of God gets put to the side. All the while, we race through life, eyes fixed on our own goals, ignoring the possibility that God might have other plans for our lives and for His kingdom. So many of our decisions may not seem to carry any eternal weight. Take, for instance, whether or not you should join the church pickleball league. Certainly this decision would have no ill effect on your life. You could even make the argument that a little more exercise would be good for you. But upon seeking the counsel of the Lord and asking for His wisdom to govern your life, you may realize that perhaps adding another thing to your already packed schedule would take more of your time and much-needed presence away from your family. The little decisions we make daily will not drastically change the course of our lives, but who we eventually become is decided not by large once-in-a-lifetime decisions but by the ones we make moment by moment, every day.

It can be hard to recognize what ripples out from our decisions. Although the effect may seem small, the continual neglect of holy counsel becomes habit-forming to the point that we claim the lordship of God but show no practical need for Him in our daily existence. Yikes.

Pride is a poison that silently and consistently renders our faith ineffectual. It tells us that we need God for all things salvation-related, of course, but when it comes to the daily goings-on of our lives, things are better left under our control. This mindset leads us to approach faith as a list of obligations, and we end up doing many Christian things but miss making a lasting impact on the kingdom of God. In elevating our plans and pursuits to be the primary focus of our existence, we become blind to the greater purpose of life and the kingdom. This attitude may not be our intention, or even where you currently find yourself. Still, pride left unchecked leads to such an end. This book got its name because pride must either be put to death within us or become the death of us. It is the tumor that must be removed to save the whole body.

How do we combat something that seems to be a universal struggle of the Christian experience? How do we address this sickness without our days being overwhelmed by the constant questioning of our motives and desires? Jesus promises us peace and joy in Him, yet this struggle seems to produce the very opposite. This question assumes a belief that more peace is found in being ignorant of pride and sin—simply living life without care until we cross into heaven. While an "ignorance is bliss" mindset may temporarily alleviate the anxieties and feelings of ineptitude that battling pride brings, Jesus wants more for you. He wants to cure you so that you can grow closer to God and experience an incredible and fulfilling life of following Him. The life Jesus has promised and planned for us is one of peace and joy. This joy is not a simulated feeling borne of ignorance but a genuine joy coming from knowing deep within who we are and where we find meaning. It is a joy that regularly draws us back to the greater perspective of His kingdom and our place in it. God created life. He knows how we should live it and the paths that lead to the greatest joy and freedom. God didn't create us to live as those who live under incredible burden. His creation is to be enjoyed, and the greatest enjoyment we can find in creation is experiencing it within the purpose and provision of God. Jesus offers us meaning that dwarfs all other pursuits, one that removes our need to be the central figure of our story. A life in which we embrace something bigger, a story beyond our own, and realize our greatest potential through accepting our created identity and purpose.

While it can be overwhelming to see how deeply the poison of pride has penetrated our souls, we can still be encouraged that an antidote exists. This antidote attacks pride at the source and eventually renders us free from the sickness that has plagued us from the beginning. Where do we find this cure? Surprisingly, we get incredible insight for our journey by looking back once more to the story of Nebuchadnezzar, the pagan king of Babylon.

What did you read that was new to you?

What can you do with this?

How can you pray through this?

Who do you need to talk to about this?

What can this look like in the church?

2

The King's Dream

Have you ever had a dream you could not shake the next day? If you are married, a better question is: has your spouse ever had a dream that affected how they felt about you the next day? In my marriage, there have been a handful of times when either myself or my wife has had to apologize to the other because of offenses we committed in a dream. Intellectually, we know the other is not to blame for such things, but that doesn't change the feelings we carry upon waking. I remember one specific morning when Mallory would barely look at me. When pressed, she told me that Dream Paul had been a jerk and she needed a little space to remember reality before going about our daily routine. It was unfair and unreasonable, but I understood. Dreams can have a power and weight that is hard to explain, so imagine how much that weight compounds when a dream is given by God. Nebuchadnezzar had already experienced such dreams when the Israelites had come to Babylon, but now, the dream he had did not depict what was to come for his kingdom, but for the king himself.

The fourth chapter of Daniel is unique to the Bible in that it is the only chapter written by a pagan. It begins the same way many epistles begin, with an introduction to the author. "King Nebuchadnezzar to all peoples, nations, and languages, that dwell in all the earth" (Dan. 4:1). King Nebuchadnezzar was the king of Babylon, the most powerful nation in the world, which became so by conquering other nations to grow its influence and domain. After defeating Egypt in the battle of Carchemish, Babylon began to assert control over Judah.

This dominion culminated in the eventual besiegement of Judah's capital, Jerusalem. As was their custom, when Babylon captured a new kingdom, they would employ time-tested practices to ensure the submission of their new subjects. Therefore, when they conquered a new region, they took steps to ensure that the people understood how completely they had been defeated. So when Babylon overtook Jerusalem, they not only defeated the armies of Jerusalem but pillaged the holy vessels from the temple and took captive the young noblemen and princes from them. In doing this, they boldly stated that both Judah's past and future were now in the hands of Babylon, to whom they would be submissive. However, Nebuchadnezzar had accumulated far more than he had anticipated in taking both the vessels and the young men. Although it seemed like the Israelites were thoroughly conquered, they remained God's people. Nebuchadnezzar had yet to encounter a living God. He had no idea the power he was encountering.

God had been clear with the Israelites that if they did not follow His commands, He would give them over to the reign of foreign kings. However, He also promised in Deuteronomy 30 that if they repented from their sins, He would return them to the land of His promise, and God keeps His promises. One of the more prominent themes of the book of Daniel is the sovereignty of God. While conquering the land and pillaging its people and possessions would make it seem like Nebuchadnezzar was in complete authority, Babylon was essentially the disciplinary arm of the Lord both against and for His people. Nebuchadnezzar would soon find out that, while he was the king of Babylon, God's sovereignty surpasses even that of the most powerful kings.

Throughout the book of Daniel, Nebuchadnezzar, much like the pharaoh of Exodus, witnessed the power of the God of the Hebrews. In the first chapters, when the king had a dream that no wise man could interpret, God spoke through Daniel to show Nebuchadnezzar its interpretation. In Daniel 3, the God of Shadrach, Meshach, and

Abednego withstood the king's blazing furnace without even so much as a trace of smoke or singed hair. In both instances, Nebuchadnezzar was perplexed and responded by giving honor to God, but though honor was given, he withheld the devotion of his heart.

How often is that our story as well? Israel had long enjoyed the provision of God in a land that provided for their needs. They had seen enemies fall and enjoyed the produce of the land time and time again, but as is often the case, when provision is plentiful, complacency takes root. They had become comfortable with the provision of God and somewhere along the way neglected to submit to His lordship. Very often, we enthusiastically accept the salvation and provision of God. We know that we cannot provide salvation for ourselves and so we readily embrace God's involvement. We praise times of seeing Him act for our benefit. When our lives become difficult or we experience situations beyond our control, we plead with God to alleviate our circumstances. But even then, we seek His intervention, not His lordship. We accept that we cannot save ourselves. We know that we need God to act for our sins to be forgiven and for our salvation, but at the same time believe we are sufficient to handle the day-to-day order of our lives. We want the salvation of God, but when it comes to our daily experience, we would rather God go along with whatever we have in mind.

It is common when reading stories like those of Daniel and his friends to identify more with the heroes of the story. We imagine ourselves speaking the truths of Daniel, standing with Shadrach, Meshach, and Abednego against the idolatrous commands of the king, or refusing to cease praying even under the threat of death at the mouths of lions. We want to believe the best of ourselves, that when put to the test, we would stand firmly and boldly against worldly foes. However, the actual condition of our hearts, as evidenced by our daily decisions and desires, paints a different picture of our aspirations. Truthfully, we don't know how we would respond in such a situation. Still, as much as we would like to identify with Daniel,

Shadrach, Meshach, and Abednego, it is in Nebuchadnezzar's heart and actions that we are reflected.

The king had experienced the power of God in inexplicable ways. He acknowledged that the God of the Hebrews had power and was to be honored and placated, but he viewed the power of God as a tool to supplement his kingdom. Nebuchadnezzar still saw himself as the ultimate and sovereign ruler of Babylon. But in the first three verses of Daniel 4, we see a drastic change in Nebuchadnezzar's view of God. It is apparent through Nebuchadnezzar's words that God finally had his full attention:

> King Nebuchadnezzar to all peoples, nations, and languages, that dwell in all the earth: Peace be multiplied to you! It has seemed good to me to show the signs and wonders that the Most High God has done for me. How great are his signs, how mighty his wonders! His kingdom is an everlasting kingdom, and his dominion endures from generation to generation (Dan. 4:1–3).

Do you see how drastically Nebuchadnezzar's perspective changed? What would happen to make the king of the most powerful nation in the world acknowledge a kingdom other than his own as everlasting? This is a very different Nebuchadnezzar than the one who raised a statue to his own glory and demanded it be worshipped. This change was not a simple understanding that Nebuchadnezzar had come to privately either; he sent this decree to "all peoples, nations, and languages that dwell in all the earth." He quite literally told the whole world about the wonders of the Most High God. This should fill us with no small amount of wonder and curiosity as to what happened to cause such a change in him. The king's transformation, while eventually bringing a drastic encounter with the justice of God, began with a dream.

One night, while the king was lounging in his house, fully content in the spoils of his wealth, he had a dream that alarmed him. Upon awakening, in his dread, the king issued a decree that all the wise men of his kingdom were to come before him to offer an interpretation. One by one, the wisdom of the wisest men in Babylon was found lacking.

One interesting thing to note is that the wise men made no attempt to interpret the dream. It was common practice at the time for dreams to be interpreted by first hearing the dream then comparing the symbols and content with past dreams. They would look to a previous dream and the events that followed to glean wisdom about the possible outcomes of the most recent dream. However, the wise men in Daniel 4 made no attempt to offer anything in the way of a possible interpretation. One probable reason is that they feared the king's wrath should they be incorrect, but another possibility is they knew that Daniel had yet to speak on the matter. Daniel had already proven successful, where they had come up short in interpreting dreams. So whether in their wisdom or fear, they may have felt it prudent to keep silent until Daniel had his say. Regardless of the reason for their inability to offer an interpretation, Daniel finally arrived on the scene:

> At last Daniel came in before me—he who was named Belteshazzar after the name of my god, and in whom is the spirit of the holy gods—and I told him the dream, saying, "O Belteshazzar, chief of the magicians, because I know that the spirit of the holy gods is in you and that no mystery is too difficult for you, tell me the visions of my dream that I saw and their interpretation" (Dan. 4:8–9).

It's interesting that, in Nebuchadnezzar's words, Daniel was one in whom was the "spirit of the holy gods." The word "holy" is a word that means, "set apart." So when Nebuchadnezzar talked of the God of Daniel, he acknowledged something different about the God that Daniel worshipped. The religious beliefs of Babylon focused on the worship of many different deities, the chief of which was the god Marduk. Even Daniel's Babylonian name, Belteshazzar, meant,

"Lady, protect the king." The "lady" refers to Bel, who is believed to be Marduk's wife. In the Babylonian belief system, the gods were to be appeased to avoid their curses, but with the God of Daniel, Nebuchadnezzar had seen a living God who was actively involved in the lives of His worshippers. Therefore, he rightly addressed Daniel's God as one who is holy or set apart from the gods of Babylon. Not only this but in his distress, Nebuchadnezzar made strides to appease God before he sought counsel. Nebuchadnezzar was desperate for understanding, and all else had failed, so he placed himself before the one God who had proven to possess a power beyond the king's comprehension. It was on this God and His servant that Nebuchadnezzar now relied to receive an understanding of his dream.

Daniel entered the king's presence, and Nebuchadnezzar told him of his dream:

> The visions of my head as I lay in bed were these: I saw, and behold, a tree in the midst of the earth, and its height was great. The tree grew and became strong, and its top reached to heaven, and it was visible to the end of the whole earth. Its leaves were beautiful and its fruit abundant, and in it was food for all. The beasts of the field found shade under it, and the birds of the heavens lived in its branches, and all flesh was fed from it. "I saw in the visions of my head as I lay in bed, and behold, a watcher, a holy one, came down from heaven. He proclaimed aloud and said thus: 'Chop down the tree and lop off its branches, strip off its leaves and scatter its fruit. Let the beasts flee from under it and the birds from its branches. But leave the stump of its roots in the earth, bound with a band of iron and bronze, amid the tender grass of the field. Let him be wet with the dew of heaven. Let his portion be with the beasts in the grass of the earth. Let his mind be changed from a man's, and let a beast's mind be given to him; and let seven periods of time pass over him. The sentence is by the decree of the watchers, the decision by the word of the holy ones, to the end that the living may know that the Most High rules the kingdom of men and gives it to whom he will and sets over it the lowliest of men.' This dream I, King Nebuchadnezzar, saw. And you, O Belteshazzar, tell me the interpretation, because

all the wise men of my kingdom are not able to make known to me the interpretation, but you are able, for the spirit of the holy gods is in you" (Dan. 4:10–18).

Imagine Nebuchadnezzar's relief when Daniel entered the room. In his previous dream, Nebuchadnezzar had been disturbed by his visions. Daniel had given an interpretation that, while not precisely favorable, had at least given the king the pride of knowing he was presiding over Babylon at its height. His previous dread had been foretold, that the empires that would come after Nebuchadnezzar's would degrade until they were completely conquered. While this would have been distressing, Nebuchadnezzar's actions, namely, building a ninety-foot-tall statue to represent his glory and the glory of Babylon, show that he was okay with the interpretation. Looking now at this dream, it is understandable that Nebuchadnezzar expected Daniel's interpretation to bring understanding and comfort. However, as the king spoke his dream to Daniel, it became more evident by Daniel's face that any hope of a favorable interpretation was in vain. Daniel's face had fallen. He was greatly troubled to the point of being alarmed. Why? Because it is a dangerous business to deliver bad news to a king, especially when that king has already shown a propensity toward harsh reactions. Seeing Daniel's face and reluctance, the king broke the silence and assured Daniel, "Let not the dream or the interpretation alarm you" (Dan. 4:19). The king wanted Daniel to know that it was okay, he could tell him everything, leaving nothing out. Daniel then tried to brace the king for what was to come: "May the dream be for those who hate you and its interpretation for your enemies" (Dan. 4:19). Having said this, Daniel then told the meaning of his dream:

> The tree you saw, which grew and became strong, so that its top reached to heaven, and it was visible to the end of the whole earth, whose leaves were beautiful and its fruit abundant, and in which was food for all, under which beasts of the field found shade, and in whose branches the birds of the heavens lived—it is

you, O king, who have grown and become strong. Your greatness
has grown and reaches to heaven, and your dominion to the ends
of the earth. And because the king saw a watcher, a holy one,
coming down from heaven and saying, 'Chop down the tree and
destroy it, but leave the stump of its roots in the earth, bound
with a band of iron and bronze, in the tender grass of the field,
and let him be wet with the dew of heaven, and let his portion
be with the beasts of the field, till seven periods of time pass over
him,' this is the interpretation, O king: It is a decree of the Most
High, which has come upon my lord the king, that you shall be
driven from among men, and your dwelling shall be with the
beasts of the field. You shall be made to eat grass like an ox, and
you shall be wet with the dew of heaven, and seven periods of
time shall pass over you, till you know that the Most High rules
the kingdom of men and gives it to whom he will. And as it was
commanded to leave the stump of the roots of the tree, your
kingdom shall be confirmed for you from the time that you know
that Heaven rules (Dan. 4:20–26).

Nebuchadnezzar would have understood the weight of a decree.
According to the law, the king could do almost anything he saw fit
to do. However, the one thing the king could not do was go back on
a decree. We see this principle at work in the decrees of King Darius
in Daniel 6 as well as in the actions of King Ahasuerus in the book of
Esther. Once a decree was set in motion, nothing, including the king's
wishes, could stop it. Decrees held authority, which could only come
from one who had the right and ability to see them carried out. Therefore, for Daniel to say this was a decree from the Most High meant
that these things would inevitably come to pass. However, in Daniel's subsequent response, we see that Daniel has affection and respect
for the king and wishes to alleviate his future suffering. He would not
dare step over the words of God. Still, he does give counsel to Nebuchadnezzar: "Therefore, O king, let my counsel be acceptable to you:
break off your sins by practicing righteousness, and your iniquities by
showing mercy to the oppressed, that there may perhaps be a lengthening of your prosperity" (Dan. 4:27). Daniel gave no hope that these

things could be avoided, but he did offer Nebuchadnezzar a way to hold off this humiliation with acts of righteousness and repentance.

There are a few insights we should glean from this.

First, when God wants to get someone's attention, He gets their attention. The Lord had decided to teach Nebuchadnezzar humility. If you remember Nebuchadnezzar's first dream, he was depicted as the leader of Babylon, the "head of gold" on the statue. The point of this dream was to communicate that all the kingdoms of man eventually crumble and fall before the eternal kingdom of God. Nebuchadnezzar's response was to erect a statue to laud the glory of Babylon, not exactly the point Daniel had tried to communicate. God then showed up again to reveal His power through the king's furnace. Still, the pride of Nebuchadnezzar survived. It is a dangerous thing to turn a deaf ear to God, as God eventually let the king know that his humiliation was no longer an option; it was now a decree. God had the king's full attention.

The second thing we understand from this is that God's justice, warnings, and punishment are meant to bring about repentance. Daniel's counsel at the end of his interpretation is for the king to drastically change the way he rules in an effort to delay the judgment of God. He tells the king to repent, to fully learn the lessons of God that had yet to take root in his heart. It is obvious that the king is being called to repentance, but the real question is this: Why is God bothering to offer any chance of repentance to this somewhat exhausting pagan king? Why bother to get Nebuchadnezzar's attention at all? Looking at Nebuchadnezzar's past and the decisions he made, it is not hard to make a case for someone deserving the wrath of God. So to offer him any kind of opportunity for being spared seems not only reckless but insulting to the people of God who had been taken captive in the name of the king. If the people of Israel, at this time, had made a list of those who were least worthy of receiving any grace and attention from God, Nebuchadnezzar's name would likely have made the top.

But for this: God's grace is exclusively given to people who don't deserve it. It is a human tendency to create a tier-based system of worthiness when it comes to favor from God. We would never claim to be worthy of God's forgiveness and provision, but we do sometimes claim to be *more* worthy than those who live in ways much further removed from God's will and direction. This is not unlike the pharisee in Luke 18.

> God's grace is exclusively given to people who don't deserve it.

Jesus tells this story:

> Two men went up into the temple to pray, one a Pharisee and the other a tax collector. The Pharisee, standing by himself, prayed thus: "God, I thank you that I am not like other men, extortioners, unjust, adulterers, or even like this tax collector. I fast twice a week; I give tithes of all that I get." But the tax collector, standing far off, would not even lift up his eyes to heaven, but beat his breast, saying, "God, be merciful to me, a sinner" (Luke 18:10–13).

When it comes to the grace of God, we are all unworthy. Therefore, the only thing that sets us apart from any other sinner in this world is not our level of worthiness but our acceptance and desire for the grace and mercy of God.

However, sometimes the grace of God looks like punishment. We're told in Hebrews, "the Lord disciplines the one he loves" (Heb. 12:6). When we find ourselves as the object of the grace of God shown in discipline, our response should be to praise God that He loves us enough to call out and discipline us. Discipline is an undeserved evidence of God's great love for us. God gives mercy to whom He pleases, and in the book of Daniel, we see Him offer grace to one whom all would see as an enemy of God. This should fill us with wonder and also with hope. For if God can give grace to the pagan king of Babylon, He most certainly can provide grace to you.

What did you read that was new to you?

What can you do with this?

How can you pray through this?

Who do you need to talk to about this?

What can this look like in the church?

3

Greatest Intentions

recently had lunch with my friend, Josh. As we ate rolls and sipped on Dr. Pepper, he began to tell me about his struggles with addiction. Within the past year Josh had come to the understanding that he was an alcoholic. By the time our entrées arrived, he had recounted several stories of nights spent drinking and the inevitable hangover and regret awaiting him the next morning. Each time he would feel a moment of clarity, in which he could see all that his addiction was stealing from both him and his family. That clarity would lead him to make promises and vow to do better, but the promises were forgotten or silenced the next time he found himself in a convenience store. After a pause Josh said, "I came to a point where I knew my intentions, regardless of how good they were, would never be enough to cure my sickness." Josh had come to the point we all need to come to. While my heart breaks for his journey, he finally arrived at an understanding that so many miss.

If you were to go to a gym in early January, or the "self-help" section of any bookstore at the same time, you would see several people with two things in common: First, an unshakable optimism that their future will be better than their present. Second, that the only thing standing in the way of the people they have always wanted to be is working harder at their goals. I don't disparage their efforts or their optimism, but as someone who has taken that route, I do wonder why those gym memberships end up canceled and those books end up collecting dust under the coffee table. That being said, if you're in the market for some great self-help books, I have plenty under my coffee table—you'll have to brush off a thick layer of dust though. But why do our optimism and our desires fail to produce lasting results? Why does it seem to be an unending, inescapable cycle, one that inevitably leads us to give up altogether? If our intentions and motivation are genuine then there must be another factor at play.

In our story, Nebuchadnezzar was warned that the judgment of God was imminent, along with an exhortation to change his ways. To give him some credit, he did try to do better. We know this because the next verses tell us more than a year had passed since his dream. "All this came upon King Nebuchadnezzar. At the end of twelve months he was walking on the roof of the royal palace of Babylon . . ." (Dan. 4:28–29). Nebuchadnezzar had spent a year diligently addressing his actions in the hope of delaying the sentence that had been imposed upon him by God. However, the decree of the Lord had been given and Nebuchadnezzar's actions eventually gave way to the condition of his heart, as we read on in the text: "The king answered and said, 'Is not this great Babylon, which I have built by my mighty power as a royal residence and for the glory of my majesty'" (Dan. 4:30). As we read this, we can shake our heads and think, *Poor prideful Nebuchadnezzar. You just couldn't keep your mouth shut.* It is easy to make judgments from the cheap seats, but Nebuchadnezzar's story is more like our own than we're comfortable with.

Nebuchadnezzar had a moment of clarity and fear that drastically changed his actions. He was passionate about becoming a new person and, in doing so, keeping the judgment of God from touching him. About four years ago, I went in, at the urging of my wife, for an annual check-up with my doctor. After the weigh-in, blood and urine tests, and the regular admonishment to lose weight and stress less, I left to continue about my life and wait for the results to come in. In truth, I was in the middle of a staff meeting when I got an email notification telling me the results were in. Opening the report, I read alarming paragraphs detailing a fatty liver, lowered kidney function, blood pressure concerns, and more. Then I did one of the more self-destructive things a person can do: I went on the internet to decipher these findings. Within an hour I was certain I had been given a death sentence. That night as I watched my children eating their dinner, I felt weighed down by my own mortality, a moment of clarity and of fear from which I decided changes needed to be made. Within a week I had a membership at a gym, I bought apparel and equipment to make me look the part of a regular gym goer, changed what I drank, and began the arduous process of counting calories throughout the day. Within a few weeks I began to lose weight and had more energy than I had experienced in a long time. I believed my life had taken a turn and would inevitably lead to me being a fit and revitalized person within the year. Writing this now four years later, I shake my head. I weigh the same as I did the day I received the results. I no longer count calories, but I do try to watch what I eat. I rarely work out, but January is coming, and the notion of a gym membership looms before me.

Moments of clarity are sometimes accompanied by the fear of consequences from our actions. These moments can instill within us a passion for change, but passions only seem to last for as long as the fear and novelty of a new routine remain. When the novelty wears off and the fear subsides, we find ourselves right back where we started— if not in a worse state than before. Something must change, but what?

How do we overcome addictions and practice regular holiness in a lasting way? Nebuchadnezzar's problem was not that he did not care about avoiding punishment, his problem was that in an effort to avoid punishment he only addressed his actions. Our sickness is not one of apathy that only requires greater effort, our sickness is rooted deep in the core of who we are. We have a sickness of the heart. Therefore, when we only address pride at the level of what we say and do, eventually the heart catches up and our true character comes out.

When we only address pride in our actions, eventually our heart catches up.

In the Gospel of Luke, Jesus says, "Out of the abundance of the heart his mouth speaks" (Luke 6:45). Our best intentions fail when we only address our actions and not our hearts. This is what happened to Nebuchadnezzar on his roof. However, the condition of the human heart is no surprise to God. God wasn't perplexed by Nebuchadnezzar's words because He already knew Nebuchadnezzar's heart.

When faced with our flaws, we address our actions because they are the easiest things to change and they give us a fast feeling of progress, but if our true struggle lies in the condition of our hearts, what hope then is there for us? How can we change something so foundational to who we are? It can feel like fighting a losing war. We're not only trying to overcome certain weaknesses in our personality, we are waging war against the core of our hearts. When faced with seemingly overwhelming odds it is tempting to give in to despair. When we see the amount of sin that pride produces in our lives, we begin to ask: *Why fight? If this is how I am no matter how hard I try, why bother going against it?* We are tired of guilt and failure to the point that it becomes easier to simply accept that this is a part of who we are. While doing so does offer momentary relief, we were made for more. It is true that God accepts us as we are. Romans tells us, "God shows his love for us in that while we were *still sinners*, Christ died for us" (Rom. 5:8, emphasis mine). However, while God does accept us as we are, He loves us too much to leave us unchanged. God desires that we would experience the joy of living out our created purpose free from the shackles of sin. Take heart, though, as the war against sin has been waged and won by Jesus. The struggles we face are the skirmishes against a foe who has already been defeated, though not yet vanquished. The fight against pride is a battle worth fighting, the pain of which is made bearable only by the taste of victory and freedom found not in the absence of a fight, but through the fight.

However, like all wars, this fight is costly. In the book *Mere Christianity*, C. S. Lewis gives an answer to the question: how much must I give to this fight? In his chapter on the difficulty or ease of the

Christian life, Lewis addresses our approach to morality. He says when we become Christians, we use our natural selves as the starting point of change. We identify the things that we deem good and bad within our desires, and we resolve to pursue the good or moral things and reject the things that are wrong, all the while holding on to hope that when the moral requirements of our faith have been met there will be enough of our natural selves left for us to pursue our plans and desires.

The problem with this way of thinking is that when we start with the desire to preserve the natural self, the result will inevitably be a life spent in constant denial of the things that we know are wrong yet still desire. This leads us to either give up in exasperation or to live a life with all the hallmarks of a good life while remaining void of any joy in our obedience. This is a far cry from what Jesus promised us when He said, "Come to me, all who labor and are heavy laden, and I will give you rest. Take my yoke upon you, and learn from me, for I am gentle and lowly in heart, and you will find rest for your souls. For my yoke is easy, and my burden is light" (Matt. 11:28–30).

If the burden of Jesus is easy, then why does a change of heart seem so heavy? When I became engaged to my wife, it was made clear to me by my future in-laws that the enjoyment of snow skiing was a prerequisite for family unity and acceptance. I exaggerate only slightly, but my father-in-law did buy several DVDs for me to learn the ins and outs of the slopes. Thankfully, I found a deep love for fresh powder and steep runs. One dreadful thing about skiing, though, is ski boots. I imagine if you asked any skier, you would find their love of skiing is evenly matched with their loathing of walking in ski boots. Ski boots are rigid, uncomfortable, and have almost no traction— which does tend to be important when walking in the snow. The walk from the car to the slopes is torturous.

During our first ski trip with our children, I found myself on such a walk while carrying my skis, one of my children's skis, poles, and a bag containing our lunches. Once I was halfway across the parking lot, I heard my son's voice saying, "Dad, can you carry my poles?" I did, but my ability to do so was far from graceful. Ski poles weigh almost nothing, but the added awkwardness and weight of one more thing was more than I had the capacity to carry skillfully.

Jesus' burden is light, but we come to Him with everything else weighing us down, and we refuse to let go of our burdens in favor of His. We try to carry a load that is both ours and His, which is far more than our capacity can stand. When we do this, it can leave us feeling like Jesus is asking too much of us. But that couldn't be further from the truth. His burden is designed for us: for He carries it with us. That is why Jesus uses the analogy of a yoke. Yokes were strapped to oxen so they would be able to carry a load together. He carries burdens with us.

In carrying His burden in this way, we are led to a path where we get to experience the joy of growth and lasting transformation. The only sustainable way to follow Jesus is to live out the words of Paul in his letter to the Ephesians,

> But that is not the way you learned Christ!—assuming that you have heard about him and were taught in him, as the truth is in Jesus, to put off your old self, which belongs to your former manner of life and is corrupt through deceitful desires, and to be renewed in the spirit of your minds, and to put on the new self, created after the likeness of God in true righteousness and holiness (Eph. 4:20–24).

God wants you to experience a transformed life. He doesn't want us to attempt to mix the oil and water of the old and new selves in an attempt to preserve them both. He wants to give us a new life in which we experience the fullness of what He has created us for. When we try to live with a foot in both camps, we are left with a half-life of both spiritual and worldly devotion that accomplishes nothing on either side. The gift of the Christian life is the ability to single-mindedly pursue a life that speaks beyond us into the eternal. Lewis gives us this encouragement:

The Christian way is different: harder, and easier. Christ says "Give me All. I don't want so much of your time and so much of your money and so much of your work: I want You. I have not come to torment your natural self, but to kill it. No half-measures are any good. I don't want to cut off a branch here and a branch there, I want to have the whole tree down. I don't want to drill the tooth, or crown it, or stop it, but to have it out. Hand over the whole natural self, all the desires which you think innocent as well as the ones you think wicked—the whole outfit. I will give you a new self instead. In fact, I will give you Myself: my own will shall become yours."[4]

King Nebuchadnezzar made efforts to change his actions, but doing so didn't come close to changing his heart. A change of heart is more costly than simply addressing outward actions. There was a beast within Nebuchadnezzar that seemed to serve him well. Pride can be a powerful ally in the building of an earthly kingdom, but when it comes to having treasures that last beyond us, pride is a sandy foundation that does not survive the storms of time.

God's grace was shown to Nebuchadnezzar in His willingness to take everything the king held dear. To strip him of his prestige and position so that he might discover a whole new world previously blocked from his view by the walls of pride he had built. When our lives are focused on our own glory, we become tunnel-visioned to the point that we cannot see the world around us. This world is full of great beauty and possibility, offering freedom and a purpose that so many can't see. The king had built walls that touched the sky, so high that even the obvious movements of God were not able to reach his heart.

For the king's pride to be conquered, first the king had to be humbled—and he was. At the utterance of his pride and self-glory, God responded to bring about the fulfillment of the warnings He gave in Nebuchadnezzar's dream:

While the words were still in the king's mouth, there fell a voice from heaven, "O King Nebuchadnezzar, to you it is spoken: The kingdom has departed from you, and you shall be driven from among men, and your dwelling shall be with the beasts of the field. And you shall be made to eat grass like an ox, and seven periods of time shall pass over you, until you know that the Most High rules the kingdom of men and gives it to whom he will." Immediately the word was fulfilled against Nebuchadnezzar. He was driven from among men and ate grass like an ox, and his body was wet with the dew of heaven till his hair grew as long as eagles' feathers, and his nails were like birds' claws (Dan. 4:31–33).

It is hard to imagine a more humiliating circumstance for a king. In a moment he went from someone recognized as one of the most powerful people in the world to one who was barely recognizable as a man. Try to see it from the perspective of the people of Babylon. Their king's power was absolute. He was worshipped in his position and then, one day, his hair grew out like feathers, his nails became like birds' claws, and he stayed in the pasture eating grass like one of the oxen. The king had been utterly humiliated.

However, through this humiliation Nebuchadnezzar's eyes were opened. We see as much in his response: "Now I, Nebuchadnezzar, praise and extol and honor the King of heaven, for all his works are right and his ways are just; and those who walk in pride he is able to humble" (Dan. 4:37). The king's words remind me of Paul's encouragement to Timothy. "It is a trustworthy statement, deserving full acceptance, that Christ Jesus came into the world to save sinners, among whom I am foremost of all" (1 Tim. 1:15, NASB1995).

The king essentially said, "Trust me, I know from experience that those who walk in pride, of which I am the worst, God is able to humble." Remember, Nebuchadnezzar sent his message out to the entire world. To the entire world he gave a detailed account of his pride and humiliation, and the crazy part is he did so joyfully—not with the anger or resentment for being humiliated that one might expect. He told the world that God's actions were right and just.

In the book of Job, Job lost everything and spent the majority of the book asking God to give him answers as to why those things happened to him. When God finally spoke, He didn't offer words of explanation or comfort, He rebuked Job for questioning Him. This scenario would be enough for many to react in anger or in an abandonment of their faith, yet Job's response to God's rebuke was: "I have uttered what I did not understand, things too wonderful for me, which I did not know. . . . I had heard of you by the hearing of the ear, but now my eye sees you; therefore I despise myself, and repent in dust and ashes" (Job 42:3, 5–6). Both Job's and Nebuchadnezzar's response to God's humiliation was one of submission, repentance, and worship, and rightfully so!

Such a reaction seems counterintuitive until you realize their responses came from a new perspective given to them by humility. The result of humility is a God-given perspective that cannot be seen through the eyes of human pride. It changes the way we view hardship, the way we view even the joys and pursuits of our life because we begin to see the picture of our existence as it fits into the larger story of God.

Pastor Louie Giglio, in a sermon, once tried to communicate the vastness of our universe.[5] In the sermon he said that the measurement used to understand the size of space is called a lightyear. It is the distance that can be covered if one were to travel at the speed of light, which is 186,000 miles per second, for an entire year. So if you were to travel at the speed of light for a year, you would cover 5.88 trillion miles. That is the size of the measuring stick needed to understand the vastness of space! If we were to cross our own galaxy at the speed of light, it would take one hundred thousand years—and that's just our galaxy. After sharing all of this, Giglio laughed and said, "I'm not trying to make you feel small. I'm trying to help you see that you are small." Our solar system, our planet, is inconsequential in our galaxy.

As you read this, you are a speck on the globe of earth, which is a small part of a solar system that is a speck in our galaxy, which is a speck in the universe. It is hard to realize the vastness of space without feeling utterly insignificant.

However, we serve a God who has placed every star in the universe. The psalmist writes, "He determines the number of the stars; he gives to all of them their names" (Ps. 147:4). That is enough to make us feel totally insignificant, until we realize that even in our insignificance, we are made significant by God. We're told in the Gospels, "Why, even the hairs of your head are all numbered" (Luke 12:7). In the Gospel of John we read, "For God so loved the world, that he gave his only Son, that whoever believes in him should not perish but have eternal life" (John 3:16).

It is true that you are completely insignificant, but for the fact that you are chosen by God and His choosing of you makes you incredibly significant. Humility is not something to make us feel trampled on and discarded; humility allows us to see what makes us significant—that we are chosen by God for great purpose which we would not be able to accomplish on our own.

So the question is, do we want the perspective and joy that humility alone can bring? Don't answer too quickly; sit with it for a moment. In fact, I encourage you to put the book down and pray through the implications of this idea. We don't need so much to change the things we do as much as we need to have our hearts transformed. It is only with a transformed heart that we will experience sustainable change. Lasting transformation is possible, but it comes at the cost of ourselves. Are you willing? Humility is a gift God gives so that we can better see and understand our place in His vastly larger story. As it is a gift of God, it can only be received from God. There is no number of well-intentioned actions that will manifest humility in your heart. Do you want the gifts that only humility can bring? If so, it will require the transformation of your heart—because from your heart, your actions will follow.

What did you read that was new to you?

What can you do with this?

How can you pray through this?

Who do you need to talk to about this?

What can this look like in the church?

4

The Antidote

When my kids were younger, we took a vacation to the great city of Omaha, Nebraska. Among the many sites we visited while there was the Omaha Zoo. I haven't been to many zoos, but Omaha's was incredible. They had various dome-like buildings representing the various habitats across the world, and while we were walking through the desert habitat we came across the enclosure of a black mamba. Through reading the informational plaques on the outside of its cage, I learned that the black mamba is one of the largest, fastest, and most venomous snakes in the world. Were you to be bitten by one you would lose the ability to speak in twenty minutes, be comatose in an hour, and dead within six hours. Pretty grim. As if that isn't bad enough, the hour between being bitten and becoming comatose is apparently filled with torturous pain. The only cure is an administration of antivenom within four hours of being bitten. Reading this information, I couldn't help but think about the desperation with which I would seek out the antivenom if I were bitten and the fear of not knowing if I could get to it in time. Standing in the Omaha Zoo then or now where I reside in Oklahoma, the fear of this snake—as it lives mostly in Africa—is completely irrational. So much so that fretting over access to the antivenom would be a bit ridiculous. Now, the account of sin and deadly pride in the book of Genesis shows us how we have been bitten by a serpent whose venom is far more deadly—not attacking the body of a person but the soul.

In Chapter 1 we discussed the reality of pride as a poison that actively deadens our souls from the inside out. But what if you didn't know you had been bitten? Imagine not realizing your soul is desperate for the antidote. As is often the case, we go through our days slowly dying because we do not realize that we have indeed been poisoned. This is why, if we are to ever successfully address pride in our lives, we must first understand that a poison lurks within us and feeds on the slow death of our souls. You, like me, are in desperate need of an antidote, and what do you think the antidote for the poison of pride could be? Dear reader, the antidote for pride is humility. I will give you a moment to catch your breath.

Humility is another word that is often hard to define. Like pride we can see the manifestations of humility in others, but what does humility look like at its root in our hearts? In both Daniel's and God's rebuke of Nebuchadnezzar there is a repeated thought. When Daniel interpreted Nebuchadnezzar's dream, he said:

> You shall be driven from among men, and your dwelling shall be with the beasts of the field. You shall be made to eat grass like an ox, and you shall be wet with the dew of heaven, and seven periods of time shall pass over you, till you *know that the Most High rules* the kingdom of men and gives it to whom he will. And as it was commanded to leave the stump of the roots of the tree, your kingdom shall be confirmed for you from the time that you *know that Heaven rules* (Daniel 4:25–26, emphasis mine).

Later when God spoke against Nebuchadnezzar, He said, "And you shall be made to eat grass like an ox, and seven periods of time shall pass over you, until you *know that the Most High* rules the kingdom of men and gives it to whom he will" (Daniel 4:32, emphasis mine). In these two sections of Scripture, we see the source of true humility: to *know* that God rules. This is the theme of the whole book of Daniel.

The word "know" is found all over Scripture. In Hebrew it is the word *yādha*,[6] which means to achieve an understanding of a fact or truth that is in keeping with its true nature. Essentially, it means to come to a true understanding of something. This is more than an intellectual understanding, which is why this word is used in the Old Testament to describe sexual relations as well. The act of sex is not merely a physical experience, it involves the opening of your soul to your partner. In this way, sex becomes an act of deep and intimate knowledge between a husband and wife. In the same way, to *yādha* a truth is to know it completely and intimately. This goes far beyond simple understanding in the mind; it's experiential and consuming. Another way to phrase this would be that *yādha* is to know something in its truest form to the point that it consumes and pushes out any competing ideology. Nebuchadnezzar was placed in a humiliating circumstance until he could completely and intimately know that God was the ruler over the kingdoms of man.

Up to that point, Nebuchadnezzar had a knowledge of God— he would have held the God of the Hebrews in high regard—yet he still saw himself as the ultimate ruler in Babylon. This is not unlike you and me. When you come to an acceptance of faith in God, it is not hard to see sunrises, sunsets, stars, and weather and think of the awesome power of God. We hear the Gospels and are thankful Jesus has nullified the power sin holds against us. We come to a point of acknowledging the loving power of God as it works for our benefit, but when it comes to the ruling of our lives, we remain firmly rooted in the belief that we are in charge. When sicknesses or crises come up, we are eager to put things in God's hands, but when circumstances are under control, we take the lordship of our lives back. At a foundational level we believe we are equipped to handle the management of our lives, and we view our faith as a seasoning that gives our lives an enjoyable flavor without being overpowering.

Nebuchadnezzar's humiliation shows us that all kings, be it kings of nations or simply the kings that we represent in our own lives, must submit to a lordship greater than their own. In 2 Samuel the Israelites demanded a king to rule them. Like many children, their one argument was that everyone else had a king and they wanted one too. God allowed this and when kings were put in place God did not step in front of their authority. It's interesting to note that when a king took his God-given authority and gave it back to God, his kingdom was successful, but when he took the reins of his kingdom and scooted God to the side, hardship wasn't far behind.

In the garden of Eden, God gave humanity its greatest gift: choice. Meaning we were granted the lordship of our lives. God continues to honor that gift. He will never force anyone to love Him or follow Him. However, this incredible gift of life can only be experienced to its fullest measure by taking that lordship and giving it back to God: to come to a place where we know both experientially and intellectually that God rules.

My son, Eli, is an incredible kid, but he is stubborn. One day I was watching him try to carry a box up the stairs. This box weighed more than he did, so I knew he had no hope of accomplishing the task. I attempted to tell him that he would need, at the very least, help from me, but he looked at me and said, "Dad, I think I've got this." What followed were five or six agonizing minutes of me watching the poor kid try every way he could think of to lift the box up the stairs. After he had exhausted both his strength and my patience, he looked back to me and said, "Yup, I'm not strong enough." I laughed, but I was also struck with a sense of familiarity.

I became the lead pastor at Lakewood Christian Church in September 2019. I knew it would be a difficult job, requiring wisdom and good leadership, and, in my hubris, I believed I had both wisdom and leadership for the task ahead of me—and in the event that I wasn't enough, God would graciously supplement. Going into 2020, I soon realized that not only did I not have enough wisdom but I had no wisdom to lead this church. Within five months of me being there, we were in the middle of a pandemic. There were so many meetings and counseling sessions with church members, elders, and staff where I realized I had nothing to offer in the way of advice or counsel. I was sinking and the feelings overwhelming me were best expressed in the words of my son: "I'm not strong enough."

My failure was the belief that God needed me to do what only I could do at Lakewood. The truth was that God was equipped to do everything He wanted to do, and, in His grace, was allowing me to be used by Him for the task. I do not have enough wisdom to do what God wants to do at the church I serve. However, God wasn't offering to supplement my wisdom; He was offering to *be* my wisdom. In his epistle, James says, "If any of you lacks wisdom, let him ask God, who gives generously to all without reproach, and it will be given him" (James 1:5). God held all the wisdom I would ever need and offered it freely, yet I had to come to a point where I knew, *yādha*, that God is the ruler of the kingdoms of man. Colossians 1 tells us:

> He is the image of the invisible God, the firstborn of all creation. For by him all things were created, in heaven and on earth, visible and invisible, whether thrones or dominions or rulers or authorities—all things were created through him and for him. And he is before all things, and in him all things hold together (Col. 1:15–17).

A life of humility happens when we surrender the lordship of our lives back to God—when we finally come to the point of knowing that we are not enough. In his commentary on the book of Galatians, Timothy Keller writes, "Ultimately, the gospel is offensive because the cross stands against all schemes of self-salvation."[7] The gospel forces us to come face-to-face with the truth that we are not enough to provide for our own salvation through any amount of good intention or righteous deeds; in the end we are still found lacking. We are okay with the idea that we need a God to save us, but we so often focus on what God has saved us from to the point that we give little thought to what God has saved us for. The ultimate goal of the gospel is not salvation, it is reconciliation. Before sin came into the world, Adam and Eve

A life of humility happens when we surrender lordship back to God.

were able to walk alongside God; they were able to join Him in His work and speak freely to Him as with a friend. Sin ended the intimacy they enjoyed. That intimacy is what God intended between Himself and His creation. Everything following the fall was intentionally appointed to bring about a reconciliation between God and His people. Salvation is an incredible gift, but it is not the end of our path; rather, it's a tool to bring about a reconciliation between us and God.

We are now living in a time when we can once again talk with God freely. We have a familiarity with God unknown to the Israelites in the time of Abraham, Daniel, and David; this is the victory of Jesus. It was for this reason that Jesus, who was equal with God, chose to be humbled. Philippians 2 tells us,

> Have this mind among yourselves, which is yours in Christ Jesus, who, though he was in the form of God, did not count equality with God a thing to be grasped, but emptied himself, by taking the form of a servant, being born in the likeness of men. And being found in human form, he humbled himself by becoming obedient to the point of death, even death on a cross (Phil. 2:5–8).

Jesus put on our flesh, accepted the cross, and took the wrath of God upon himself because He wanted to be reconciled to us. This gift, however, lavishes on us another grace of God—that we get to be transformed to be like Him.

Jesus tells us in the Gospel of Matthew: "If anyone would come after me, let him deny himself and take up his cross and follow me. For whoever would save his life will lose it, but whoever loses his life for my sake will find it" (Matt. 16:24–25). In following Jesus we are invited on a journey of transformation, but far too often we approach the journey with our own list of conditions and exceptions. Essentially, we build a wall around ourselves with the understanding that we will be devoted to whatever Jesus has for us, up to a certain point—so long as He beckons us no further than the walls we've made. The call of Christ is to give Him the entirety of our lives, so that He may tear down the walls of our constructed life for us to discover true life in their place. When Jesus told people to take up their cross, He made it clear that the journey of following Him would cost them their lives, and the same is true for us. He also gave the promise that the cost of our lives is a small sum in comparison with the life He has in store for us.

The Christian life is one of transformation, but transformation is only possible through God at work in us and through us. This means that, if we are to truly uncover the purpose of our salvation, it must come at the cost of ourselves. Romans 12:1 tells us to present our bodies as a living sacrifice, holy and acceptable to God. We are saved by God so we can surrender our lives to His lordship for His glory and our good. It is through relinquishing control that we discover the truest experience and potential of our lives. God has given us every reason to trust Him, but we will never experience the reflected life of Jesus' humility until we come to a place of knowing God rules and fully trusting in His lordship. This knowledge yields a humility with nothing to prove, no expectation to be self-made, and every reason to rest in the accomplishments of God done around us and through us.

I recently read an article written by Mike Donehey,[8] the lead singer for the band Tenth Avenue North. In the article he told a story of when their band was about to play at a festival. In their van, the band gathered to pray over their set. Their prayers comprised much of what we would pray in that situation: "God, please use us," "God, please speak through our music." During the prayer Mike opened his eyes and saw the other artists, many of whom were more known than they were, and began to wonder what it would be like to have *their* following and influence. It then hit him as if God spoke directly with a question: "What if I want to use someone else?" This was transformational for Mike, changing his prayer from, "God, use me," to, "God, please move." It's a subtle shift, but it is one that makes all the difference in the world. When we come to a knowledge of God's sovereignty, we cease to care whether we are the central character or the one in control. Our greatest desire is for God to move, and we stand ready to celebrate any time we see or sense His movement around us. In this we live out the words of the apostle Paul: "Therefore I will boast all the more gladly of my weaknesses, so that the power of Christ may rest upon me" (2 Cor. 12:9). True humility is one where we would willingly put our failures on display for the world if it would mean that the glory of Christ could be proclaimed, where we would rather Christ be known for His grace in our failures than we be known for our accomplishments.

It is a long journey of humility, and the first and foundational step is to know God rules.

What did you read that was new to you?

What can you do with this?

How can you pray through this?

Who do you need to talk to about this?

What can this look like in the church?

5

The Air of Heaven

once heard an illustration by Pastor Rick Atchley[9] where he talked about whales. Most everyone has seen a video or picture of whales breaching the surface of the water. Whales live most of their lives underwater. Blue whales can dive to depths of over one thousand feet! Even the whale's vision is better underwater. However, as much as a whale is at home underwater, for its own survival, every fifteen to thirty-five minutes it must breach the surface and breathe the air from above; this is the only way for the blue whale to survive the depths below.

Right now, we see this world better than we can see the heavenly realms. The things around us seem concrete. When we think of our cars, houses, workplaces, even our churches, they seem more real than the spiritual world which we can only understand in abstract terms. But the truth is that the spiritual world is far more true, far more real, and will far outlive our physical world. Paul tells the church in Corinth as much in his letters, "We look not to the things that are seen but to the things that are unseen. For the things that are seen are transient, but the things that are unseen are eternal" (2 Cor. 4:18).

The reason we have a tainted view of our world is because, not unlike whales, we see better here. This is the world we experience daily, so we use our concrete understanding to perceive abstract things. This is why, when scripture talks about heaven and hell, it uses images like streets of gold and a lake of fire, things we understand are used to describe the indescribable.

The pivot point for Nebuchadnezzar's story was not when his sanity was taken from him; Nebuchadnezzar's moment of realization and change happened at the end of his affliction:

> At the end of the days I, Nebuchadnezzar, lifted my eyes to heaven, and my reason returned to me, and I blessed the Most High, and praised and honored him who lives forever, for his dominion is an everlasting dominion, and his kingdom endures from generation to generation; all the inhabitants of the earth are accounted as nothing, and he does according to his will among the host of heaven and among the inhabitants of the earth; and none can stay his hand or say to him, "What have you done?" At the same time my reason returned to me, and for the glory of my kingdom, my majesty and splendor returned to me. My counselors and my lords sought me, and I was established in my kingdom, and still more greatness was added to me. Now I, Nebuchadnezzar, praise and extol and honor the King of heaven, for all his works are right and his ways are just; and those who walk in pride he is able to humble (Dan. 4:34–37).

Nebuchadnezzar's humiliation ended when he lifted his eyes to heaven and, finally, from that perspective he knew in his heart that God rules—which led him to worship God, not as one of the many deities to be placated but as the one true God and ruler of a kingdom which will endure forever. Nebuchadnezzar came to the point of *yādha* at last.

We strive toward the same thing, perceiving our lives through the lens of God's lordship. Do you see the freedom such a perspective offers? Which of our problems are overwhelming when God is the true leader of our lives? His kingdom is everlasting, His grace is sufficient for our needs, His love does not fade with our faithfulness or lack thereof. When we know God rules, it gives us a humble peace transcending frail human understanding. Philippians 4 tells us: "Do not be anxious about anything, but in everything by prayer and supplication with thanksgiving let your requests be made known to God.

And the peace of God, which surpasses all understanding, will guard your hearts and your minds in Christ Jesus" (Phil. 4:6–7).

So when we're faced with the worst of this world, when our worry tempts us to take the lordship of our lives back into our own hands, we can remember our lives are in the hands of a sovereign and sufficient God. Romans 8 says, "And we know that for those who love God all things work together for good, for those who are called according to his purpose" (Rom. 8:28). When God is the Lord of our lives, we become free to move within His purposes knowing that He is in control, and we can recite with confidence what Paul says only two verses later in Romans 8:31: "What then shall we say to these things? If God is for us, who can be against us?"

Knowing God rules gives us a humble peace transcending frail human understanding.

This is the perspective God offers us through humility, and it sounds well and good, but how can we attain it? How can we steward our mindset toward humility? In the fourth chapter of Revelation, John received a vision from God. In the following chapters, alarming and confusing things were revealed to John, but before John was shown any of those things, he saw a glimpse of the throne room of God. He was given a taste of heaven to serve as a context—and reminder—for what came next in the vision.

Much like a whale breaking through the surface to breathe the air from above, we too must break through the surface of our temporary reality to breathe in the air of heaven. Scripture and prayer, essential for the Christian life, realign our loves and renew our perspectives so we can see our transient world clearly through the eyes of heaven. Timothy Keller in his book on prayer said, "What is prayer, then, in the fullest sense? Prayer is continuing a conversation that God has started through his Word and his grace, which eventually becomes a full encounter with him."[10] This is why both Scripture and prayer must walk together: they inform each other and bring about a full encounter with God. Keller goes on to say, "Prayer turns theology into experience. Through it we sense his presence and receive his joy, his love, his peace and confidence, and thereby we are changed in attitude, behavior, and character."[11] Go often to Scripture, pray through its pages, and let it do its work in your soul. Breathe the air of heaven.

In the five years I have been preaching at Lakewood, I have written and delivered over two hundred sermons, not all of which were home runs. I look back on some of the sermons I gave in my first year and I am humbled that the church put up with my clumsy preaching! However, there have been several seasons in the past five years when I have struggled in my own personal study of Scripture. Opening the Bible at home began to feel like I was bringing my work home with me. At its worst, I could not read any portion of Scripture without thinking through how I would preach it. This could be dismissed as a passion for communicating the Word, but the danger of it to me was that I was actively preaching the Word without ever letting the Word preach to me. I began to read Scripture with a curiosity and desire to preach, but my desire to understand and be changed by the words began to take precedence. From this emerged a partnership between prayer and study where the Word of God came to life for me. I was experiencing the Scriptures in a way I had yet to experience them. When I read passages, I would imagine the original audience reading them for the first time and then I would see the words travel throughout the generations to now speak to me and eventually our church. In my heart I felt and finally knew the truth of Hebrews 4: "The word of God is living and active, sharper than any two-edged sword, piercing to the division of soul and of spirit, of joints and of marrow, and discerning the thoughts and intentions of the heart" (Heb. 4:12). While this is still a struggle for me, I now have the foundation of this truth and the experience of His Word to be able to stop and see the reality of what I am doing. When we go to Scripture through prayer, our heads break through the surface of our worldly waters and we are able to breathe the air of heaven which is our life source as we swim through the depths of this world.

I am the youngest of three siblings, all boys. If at this point you feel the need to get on your knees and say a prayer of deliverance for my mother, your prayers may be too late—but they are nevertheless appreciated. While I experienced my fair share of abuse at the hands of my older brothers, it always seemed to rise in frequency during the summer months when we were at home with nothing to do except chores.

One particular summer day we were invited to go to our neighbor's house to swim. Growing up in the Church of Christ, we had a predisposition toward baptism and therefore, the main portion of our time in that pool was spent doing a dunk contest. If you are not familiar with dunk contests, the rules are fairly simple: you pick the weakest person in the pool—that would be me—and proceed to force their entire body underwater as many times as you can. I never won these contests, but on that day both of my brothers made me their target. While we were in the deep end of the pool, one of my brothers grabbed me and shoved me under the water. As I came up to take a breath, however, I was grabbed by my other brother who did the same. The problem here was that when I opened my mouth to take a breath, water came in instead of air. Before I knew it, I was once again forced under the surface. At this point panic set in. Frantically, I tried to swim to the surface, but before I could get there, a foot connected with my shoulder and pushed me once again toward the bottom. My lungs, still heavy with the water of my previous attempt to breathe, now screamed for air with a desperation that only those who have been in this situation could appreciate. Finally, my face broke the surface of the water, and I was able to cough and breathe in air that only moments before I had taken for granted. The cries that came after were ones of relief and horror at what I had just gone through, all while my brothers begged me not to tell our mother.

The problem with the air of heaven is that we don't know how desperate we are for it. When we spend enough time submerged in the culture of our world, we begin to adapt to our surroundings. Dependence on God is replaced by dependence on ourselves, The worship of God is replaced by the worship of finances, entertainment, food, or any number of things that seem to promise fulfillment. In our attempts to make our lives in this world as comfortable as possible, our ultimate goals are revealed. In doing this we place ourselves as the lords of our lives. We elevate our desires and control to a place rightly belonging to God and we begin to drown in a pool of pride—all at the hands of our own selves. Truthfully, we are the little kid in the deep end of the pool desperate for his next breath—only we forget how much we need oxygen and neglect fighting to reach the surface altogether.

In the Old Testament, one of the most common rebukes given to the Israelites was that they forgot their God.[12] It was for this reason that God set up feasts, celebrations, altars, and stones so that the people would regularly see them and remember what He had done. This is why Jesus during the Last Supper set up another meal of communion, so that we would, "Do this in remembrance of [Him]" (Luke 22:19).

We tend to forget what we don't choose to remember regularly. Whether it is going to the gym, attending church, or habitual study and prayer, if we miss it often enough, we stop missing it. Then if it continues for long enough, we forget why it was ever vital to begin with. Our remembrance of our desperate need for God is as essential for our soul as air is for our body. We need to breathe the air of heaven. We need to be in the presence of God regularly because it is only in the consistent presence of God that our pride will finally be overpowered. Pride cannot stand the presence of God.

Only in the consistent presence of God will our pride finally be overpowered.

So often in Scripture, when angels appeared before people, their first words were, "Do not be afraid." I've wondered why the first reaction to seeing the glory of heaven would be fear. I'm sure that seeing an angelic being suddenly appear would be enough to cause anyone to tremble, but I also believe the fear goes deeper than a reaction to what the eyes see. When we find ourselves in the presence of true holiness, we come to see ourselves in an unbiased light. We see past our intentions to the true state of our hearts and inevitably to our sin and pride. We are laid bare before the Holy God. Read the words of the prophet Isaiah:

> To whom then will you compare me, that I should be like him? says the Holy One. Lift up your eyes on high and see: who created these? He who brings out their host by number, calling them all by name; by the greatness of his might and because he is strong in power, not one is missing. Why do you say, O Jacob, and speak, O Israel, "My way is hidden from the LORD, and my right is disregarded by my God"? Have you not known? Have you not heard? The LORD is the everlasting God, the Creator of the ends of the earth. He does not faint or grow weary; his understanding is unsearchable. He gives power to the faint, and to him who has no might he increases strength. Even youths shall faint and be weary, and young men shall fall exhausted; but they who wait for the LORD shall renew their strength; they shall mount up with wings like eagles; they shall run and not be weary; they shall walk and not faint (Isa. 40:25–31).

When we stand before God, we are overwhelmed by how we do not measure up. It is intimidating to intentionally stand in places where we know we have no right. Yet we are told that God gives power to the faint and strength to the weak. God is not surprised by our struggles and depravity, and He is able and willing to deliver us. With pride being such an integral and insidious part of our character, the road ahead can seem like an endless battle with little to no chance of victory. But when we regularly enter the presence of God, when we regularly breathe the air of heaven, our pride is diagnosed and torn away. This happens over and over again, which would seem exhausting, if not for the fact that we serve a God who promises to renew our strength and give us wings like eagles so we can run and not grow weary, walk and not faint. His breath sustains us; it is the air of heaven giving us perspective and strength to continue. Breathe the air of heaven. Breathe it often and deeply.

We breathe the air of heaven by stepping regularly into the throne room of God through study, worship, and prayer. While enormously valuable for us to do on our own, the air of heaven is most fully experienced within community. C. S. Lewis argues that only through community can we come to know each other and ourselves in any real and full way. He says, "In each of my friends there is something that only some other friends can fully bring out. By myself I am not large enough to call the whole man into activity; I want other lights than my own to show all his facets."[13] Lewis goes on to say that the loss of a friend not only takes the friend away, but also what the friend brought out in others.

We are meant to experience life within community. Even God exists within the community of the Trinity. If we cannot even come to understand each other fully without community, how much more do we need community to understand the character of God? When we enter the presence of God together through prayer, worship, and the reading of the Word, we learn more about God, each other, and ourselves.

It can be intimidating to be so vulnerable before God and with others. One of the more vulnerable prayers in Scripture is found in Psalm 139. In the last two verses, David invites God to search and know his entire heart. The thought alone causes me to shudder because I know what lurks in some of the darker corners of my heart, but David then takes it further by asking God to point out everything offending in him as he is led by God to the everlasting.

At some level I still believe I can hide my worst from God. Maybe it's because I have become so good at hiding it from others, but

David's invitation in Psalm 139 is to do away with all veils so his sinful condition can be fully seen. It is not difficult to understand how God can and does see the entirety of our hearts, but the idea of sharing that level of intimacy with others is daunting. We would maybe be willing to reach such a level of intimacy as what David expressed in the Psalm, but our argument soon becomes, *Well, it was between David and God, so there is no reason for me to involve anyone else.*

First, David wrote an entire Psalm about his remorse over committing adultery with Bathsheba and then assigned it to be sung by a choir! David was not in the habit of hiding his faults. Secondly, we are told in Scripture how we are meant to confess our sins to God for forgiveness, but that our healing comes when we confess to each other. It is a terrifying yet necessary thing to be vulnerable with others. Timothy Keller says, "To be loved but not known is comforting but superficial. To be known and not loved is our greatest fear. But to be fully known and truly loved is, well, a lot like being loved by God. It is what we need more than anything. It liberates us from pretense, humbles us out of our self-righteousness, and fortifies us for any difficulty life can throw at us."[14] God calls us into a deep level of community with Himself and with others—a place where the air of heaven is breathed regularly, pride is broken down, purpose is discovered and rediscovered, and a journey is embarked upon together.

To close this, I encourage you to take a step further: meet with a Christian brother or sister to read and pray through the words of David's prayer. Consider the implications of the psalm. Think about what it would look like if invoked in your lives. Share with each other and commit to praying for each other. This is but one step in a long journey where the road is not always visible. In his classic book, *The Lord of the Rings*, Tolkien writes, "It's a dangerous business, going out your door. You step onto the road, and if you don't keep your feet, there's no knowing where you might be swept off to."[15] We don't always know where this road goes, but we do know the destination is more than worthy of the difficulty of the trip. Therefore, breathe deep the air of heaven and step onto the road alongside the community of believers.

> *Search me, God, and know my heart;*
> *test me and know my anxious thoughts.*
> *See if there is any offensive way in me,*
> *and lead me in the way everlasting*
> (Ps.139:23–24, NIV).

What did you read that was new to you?

What can you do with this?

How can you pray through this?

Who do you need to talk to about this?

What can this look like in the church?

PART TWO

The Journey

6

A Journey Without an End

I n contemplating the fight against pride, we must come to understand that pride is not defeated on a single battlefield in one moment. The fight against pride is a journey that covers the span of our lives on which we will face roadside skirmishes along the way. Therefore, to commit to overcoming pride in our lives is to step onto the road for a long and fruitful journey filled with struggle, purpose, and joy.

As I write this, my wife and I are planning a trip for the summer. Our plan is to hook our small camper (still very glad we got one!) up to our car and travel across the country for fifteen days to visit ten different national parks. It will be seven people in a small camper for fifteen days and now, before doing such a thing, we think it is a great idea. Time will tell if it is hubris speaking, but in the meantime pray for us. We will be back by the time this book is released, but still, prayers are appreciated. One of our favorite aspects of the trip is that it isn't focused on where we're going. Not the particular destination but the journey and the memories it will create are the purposes of our trip.

In the last chapter, we spoke about stepping onto the road for a long journey of self-realization and transformation. When I tell my children to put their shoes on, one of the first questions I hear is, "Where are we going?" It's natural for us to want to know our destination before committing to the journey, and while the destination is important, often our fixation on the destination makes us impatient in the present moment and during the journey getting there.

When our children were younger, my wife and I were told on numerous occasions how the days may be long, but the years are short. We had a fifteen-month-old and a newborn. The mixture of dirty diapers, crying, and no sleep made us long for the days to be shorter. Now that our children are far beyond diapers with the oldest beginning to drive, we finally understand what those well-meaning parents were trying to communicate. We love this season of our kids' lives, but we do look back with remorse at all the days we wished away longing for the next stage when they were little babies. We wish we could go back to soak up those moments when our child's greatest desire was to be held by us, but time doesn't work that way. So now we commit to being present in the current moment and season, to enjoy who our kids are and appreciate who they are becoming, because we have come to realize that the journey of life is a gift we should treasure.

The same can and should be said for the journey of faith. Through Jesus our destination has been set. We have been saved, which means our destination is heaven, but salvation affords us the opportunity to be continually reconciled to God as we are transformed in His likeness. In the book of Hebrews, we read, "Therefore let us leave the elementary doctrine of Christ and go on to maturity, not laying again a foundation of repentance from dead works and of faith toward God" (Heb. 6:1). The doctrine of Christ is salvation and repentance, and the author of Hebrews is telling us that if we want to pursue maturity and follow Christ, we must leave these things? It seems counterintuitive. We come to church and sing songs praising God for salvation, I have preached many times about salvation, yet sometimes we struggle to believe we are saved. How can we leave salvation and repentance behind? To understand this passage, it is helpful to view it from the perspective of relationship.

I've been married to my wife, Mallory, for seventeen years. I know this because she had our anniversary engraved on the inside of my wedding ring to make sure I wouldn't forget. Smart woman. But what if for all these seventeen years I couldn't get past our wedding day? What if every morning I got up and frantically searched for our marriage certificate, looked through the pictures in our album, and watched our wedding video to prove to myself we were in fact married? What if when we argued, I became insecure about the validity of our vows? What if I spent seventeen years focusing on the insecurity of our marriage? I would still be married, but I would have missed out on so much that a marriage is supposed to be—not to mention driven my wife crazy. I am married, I know that, and I am assured of my wife's love and devotion to me. When I see our wedding pictures, I'm not filled with anxiety and insecurity, I'm filled with fondness and nostalgia for the life we have shared. I remember times of affection, times of anger, times of sadness, and times of joy. Surprisingly, it is the more difficult times that have brought us closer together.

Relationships cannot thrive if they are built on a foundation of insecurity. John tells us in his epistle, "There is no fear in love, but perfect love casts out fear" (1 John 4:18). How often in your life as a Christian have you had to deal with the insecurities surrounding your salvation? How often have you heard the assurances of salvation in Scripture and thought that somehow your sin had disqualified you? How often when you think of heaven and judgment are you overcome with fear? This is what the author of Hebrews addresses. If you have confessed Jesus as Lord, repented from your sins, and put Him on in baptism then you are saved! Romans tells us, "There is therefore now no condemnation for those who are in Christ Jesus" (Rom. 8:1). God tells Paul in 2 Corinthians, "My grace is sufficient for you" (2 Cor. 12:9). Throughout all Scripture one truth is evident: God keeps His promises. He is faithful and we can take Him at His word.

Hebrews 6 calls us to never get over that fact. May we never get over Jesus' sacrifice for our salvation and reconciliation. I'm still not over the fact that Mallory chose to marry me. I like to joke that the beauty of my wife is such that when people see us standing together, they automatically assume I have a great personality. We are not intended to get over our salvation, but we are called to move on to maturity from the foundation of our salvation. Our journey is one of being transformed to be more and more like Jesus until we reach the destination of being reconciled to God for eternity. The journey is a gift.

However, I would like to offer a quick word on repentance. The word "repent" is taken from the Greek word *metanoeō*,[16] which means to change one's mind. The root of this word comes from: "meta,"[17] meaning after or behind, and *noeō*,[18] meaning to perceive with the mind or ponder. When we put all these together, we get a practical definition of repentance—that it is when we come to a point of belief that leads us to examine our lives, our loves, our aspirations, and our decisions. We then hold our lives up in comparison to the ways and promises of God and we choose to change our minds and accept that the ways of God are better than our own. This is a necessary step in claiming Jesus as our Lord, for if we believe He is the Lord, then belief in Him requires holding the complimentary belief that His way for our lives is better than ours. We don't just long for the salvation of Jesus, we long for the lordship of Jesus because His path is the only way we will experience transformation.

While repentance is a necessary conclusion in coming to believe in Jesus and claim Him as Lord, it is also something that happens as a regular part of our lives with Jesus. Jesus accepts and saves us exactly as we are, but He loves us too much not to call us to change and grow as we follow Him. However, the nature of growth is that it always comes with pain. In his book *Leadership Pain*, Samuel Chand repeats the same notion in every chapter, "You will only grow to the threshold of your pain."[19] Growth causes pain, whether it is the physical pain of growth in a child, the pain of muscles tearing down when exercising, or the mental and spiritual pain of overcoming past sins and adopting a new worldview. However, while growth is painful, it is always worthwhile, and its pains are made bearable by the exceeding joy of feeling the old self fall away and the new self emerge.

Consider Nebuchadnezzar's story: He went through incredible pain, failure, and public humiliation. As a king who was personally invested in the people's perception of him, for the king then to end up as a laughingstock eating grass in a field with livestock would have been the epitome of humiliation. Yet, at the conclusion of his story, he did not express any anger or resentment for the path he took; he only expressed gratitude for where it brought him. We must come to accept that failure is a part of our path. The path to humility and transformation is filled with painful missteps and failures; this is why repentance is central for us. It allows us to ponder what led us to fail and to, once again, acknowledge Jesus' way as better than our own and continue in our walk with Him.

I once went to a conference where Andy Stanley was one of the speakers. Out of all the insights he shared, the most profound for me was when he said, "Embrace failure because you learn almost nothing when you win." Jesus has no intention or expectation that you will be able to walk the path of righteousness perfectly. Through His sacrifice and resurrection, He can cover not just the sins of your old life, but the struggles and failures of your life now as well. The gift of the cross is that we can now pursue a transformed life without being crushed by our failures.

This is why Paul exclaims in 1 Corinthians, "'O death, where is your victory? O death, where is your sting?' The sting of death is sin, and the power of sin is the law. But thanks be to God, who gives us the victory through our Lord Jesus Christ" (1 Cor. 15:55–57). Jesus has taken away the one weapon Satan could use against us. We no longer stand accused and guilty before God; our identity as unworthy sinners has been replaced with a new one: redeemed. Because of Jesus, our sins and failures no longer mean condemnation. Instead, they are opportunities to learn and grow as we cling more closely to

Jesus who carries our burden with us. The mile markers on the path to humility and transformation are written in pain. Grow your threshold by learning and moving in repentance from failure toward grace.

The battle to overcome pride is a journey that takes a lifetime. I don't know where you are in your struggle against pride. To many, if not most, the journey looks like an unscalable mountain. We see tendrils of pride curling around our hearts and swirling in the background of our conversations, reactions, and ambitions. Even when we do seemingly selfless things, there is still a voice whispering *our* goodness in hopes that someone will notice. The apostle Paul expressed the reality of this struggle in Romans 7. Take a moment to read this. Do you feel the angst of his words?

> For I know that nothing good dwells in me, that is, in my flesh. For I have the desire to do what is right, but not the ability to carry it out. For I do not do the good I want, but the evil I do not want is what I keep on doing. Now if I do what I do not want, it is no longer I who do it, but sin that dwells within me. So I find it to be a law that when I want to do right, evil lies close at hand. For I delight in the law of God, in my inner being, but I see in my members another law waging war against the law of my mind and making me captive to the law of sin that dwells in my members. Wretched man that I am! Who will deliver me from this body of death (Rom. 7:18–24).

How can we overcome such a present force in our lives? Mercifully, Paul does not end on an exclamation of despair. In the very next sentence, he exclaims with even more vigor the praise of our deliverance: "Thanks be to God through Jesus Christ our Lord" (Rom. 7:25). It is true to say that, left to our own devices, the mountain of pride cannot be conquered, but we do not climb alone. In the Gospel of Matthew, Jesus tells His disciples, "Truly, I say to you, if you have faith like a grain of mustard seed, you will say to this mountain, 'Move from here to there,' and it will move, and nothing will be impossible for you" (Matt. 17:20). We serve a God who can move the mountains standing in our way. In the next chapter, we are going to talk about the help that we receive from God, but for now, find peace in knowing that He is with you in the fight and it is a fight worth fighting.

Our struggle against pride is one we will have to contend with for the entirety of our lives. We will experience victories, but the enemy thinks he is not yet vanquished as he slinks to the edges of the battlefield, waiting for the opportunity to raise a new attack. This is why our fight doesn't end. We must be vigilant because we have an enemy that is unrelenting. In his epistle, Peter says, "Be sober-minded; be watchful. Your adversary the devil prowls around like a roaring lion, seeking someone to devour. Resist him" (1 Pet. 5:8–9).

In our lives we will walk from battle to battle, waging war against pride. Over the years, I have had the opportunity to speak to several friends and church members about their struggles with addiction. In talking with my previously mentioned alcoholic friend, I once asked, "Will there ever be a point at which you consider yourself healed?" He gave a somber smile and said, "No, my fight against alcohol is one I have to take day by day, every day." In the Alcoholics Anonymous Big Book, they put it this way, "We are not cured of alcoholism. What we really have is a daily reprieve contingent on the maintenance of our spiritual condition."[20] In the war against pride, we will experience victories, but they are only reprieves. Our greatest comfort in the fight against pride is to cling to Jesus, to breathe the air of heaven, and to know we are fighting alongside the God who is sovereign over all.

Our greatest comfort in the fight against pride is to cling to Jesus.

The title of this chapter is a bit of a misnomer. It is true that our journey does not end, but our fight will. Within each of us resides an eternal soul. Our journey with God will continue to be written long after our time on this earth is over. So while we will fight the battle against pride for the rest of our lives, God has promised that there will come a time when our enemies will be utterly defeated and vanquished. It is depicted in the revelation of John:

> And when the thousand years are ended, Satan will be released from his prison and will come out to deceive the nations that are at the four corners of the earth, Gog and Magog, to gather them for battle; their number is like the sand of the sea. And they marched up over the broad plain of the earth and surrounded the camp of the saints and the beloved city, but fire came down from heaven and consumed them, and the devil who had deceived them was thrown into the lake of fire and sulfur where the beast and the false prophet were, and they will be tormented day and night forever and ever (Rev. 20:7–10).

Satan's defeat is sure. The victory of God is inevitable. In our fight against pride, we have the promise that our fight will end in ultimate victory and our journey with God will continue. While the fight may seem overwhelming, remember that your journey does not end on the battlefield. We will fight pride for the rest of our lives, and through our battles we will gain humility as we are continually transformed. We will have seasons of reprieve, but pride is an enemy we will face regularly. It is daunting to think of fighting for forty, fifty, or sixty years, but, put into the context of our journey, sixty years is nothing compared to the billions and billions of years we will be with God in heaven.

Romans 8 tells us, "For I consider that the sufferings of this present time are not worth comparing with the glory that is to be revealed to us" (Rom. 8:18). Through humility we are able to put our struggles into the perspective of God's larger picture, which gives us a hope and expectation of our deliverance. C. S. Lewis concludes his series, *The Chronicles of Narnia*, with these words: "All their life in this world and all their adventures had only been the cover and the title page: now at last they were beginning Chapter One of the Great Story which no one on earth has read: which goes on forever: in which every chapter is better than the one before."[21]

With the hope of heaven set securely in our minds, may we fight with endurance to achieve the transformation of our souls and the renewal of our minds to the point that, when we finally bid farewell to this earth, we can with confidence and honesty repeat the words Paul said at the end of his life: "I have fought the good fight, I have finished the race, I have kept the faith" (2 Tim. 4:7). Fight hard but know you do not fight alone. God is our help.

What did you read that was new to you?

What can you do with this?

How can you pray through this?

Who do you need to talk to about this?

What can this look like in the church?

7

Help Along the Way

For most of my life, I have enjoyed a love for airplanes. There is something attractive about the idea of being in control of a machine with the power to defy the laws of gravity. I'm sure you remember something about me loving the idea of being able to control a machine with blades spinning at a terrifying speed. Well, what can I say? Six years ago, I had the opportunity to take a discovery flight with a flight instructor. The purpose of a discovery flight is to give an aspiring pilot an opportunity to go up in a plane, take the controls for a bit, receive some instruction, and ask questions about the specifics of flying. It had been a dream of mine for some time, so when the day arrived, I was excited. When we got to the airport, I met the instructor and we walked around the plane talking about its control surfaces and noting the different things which must be checked before takeoff. Once in the cockpit, I learned about the different gauges, switches, and controls of the plane, then at last it was time to take to the skies.

As the engine sputtered to life, I felt its vibrations through the controls. My heart raced as the instructor nudged the throttle and directed me to take the plane out to the taxiway. We spent the next fifteen minutes practicing turns and breaking before he told me to take the plane to the far side of the airport so he could talk me through all the preflight checks that must be completed before takeoff. One thing you need to know about me, for the purposes of this story, is that I am terrified of heights. I know, a fear of heights and a love of flying do not normally coexist well, but I was determined to overcome my fears in order to live out my dream.

Once all the checks were completed, the instructor looked at me and said, "Okay, what we're going to do now is simulate a landing. We're going to go out on the runway, gather a bunch of speed, and then slow down as if we had landed. Sound good?" Nodding my assent, we pulled out onto the runway. At his instruction, I pushed the throttle all the way in, and we began to pick up speed. Halfway down the runway the instructor told me, "It's getting a little bumpy. Go ahead and pull back on the stick a bit." Not daring to question him, I pulled back on the stick and the plane launched into the air. I hadn't expected this, and my reaction took the form of screaming something to the effect of, "We're in the air!" to which he replied, "Yes, that's what this thing does. Go ahead and take us up to two thousand feet."

With shaking hands and a heartbeat I could feel in my ears, I continued to climb. Once at altitude, we practiced turning, ascents, and descents until he was satisfied I had the basics down. He then asked me, "Do you know where the airport is?" It may sound far-fetched, but with all the turns and my focus primarily on the controls, I had lost my bearings and had no idea where the airport was. I looked out the windows to the left and right and saw roads and trees, but no airport. Finally, I admitted to the instructor that I had no idea where the airport was. He chuckled and said, "It's right in front of us, which is good because it's time to land." Raising myself up in the seat, I looked out of the window and, sure enough, there was the airport. The instructor then took me through the principles of landing—how you decrease altitude by decreasing the power and the importance of watching the speed. He finished his instructions and asked me if I understood. I said, "Yes." The instructor's next words were perhaps the most terrifying words I had heard up to that point in my life.

He said, "Okay, I'm dead, land the plane." This was not an expected or welcomed pronouncement, to which I responded with a barely intelligible shout of a panicked, "What?" Again, he said, "I'm dead, land the plane."

I was almost beside myself with panic, but I began to follow the steps I had been told in landing the plane. Terrifyingly, as I pulled back the throttle the plane began to descend. I knew it was what was supposed to happen when landing, but the sight of the ground slowly getting closer filled me with a sense of imminent doom. I kept glancing at the instructor's hands, willing them to take the controls, but they remained firmly in his lap. I continued to direct the plane slowly downward until I finally felt the tires screech against the pavement, to which the instructor exclaimed, "Well, you only bounced once! Go ahead and take us to the hangar."

After putting the plane away, I walked out of the hangar with mixed emotions. My whole body was shaking, and I was filled with a mixture of excitement, accomplishment, adrenaline, and fury. In that plane, granted there were only two of us, I was the least qualified person to attempt a landing. However, my fear came from the mistaken belief that whatever happened next was solely in my hands. I felt isolated and I resented the pilot for getting me into such a circumstance in the first place. I felt frustrated because it was not what I had signed up for.

The Christian life is difficult. When Jesus tells us to take up our crosses and follow Him, He's not inviting us to a weekend retreat at an all-inclusive resort. The road ahead is tough. We need to understand the reality of the cost of following Jesus. We need to understand what we're signing up for. The book of Hebrews was written to Jewish Christians, some of whom, having grown weary of persecution, had begun to consider leaving their faith in Jesus and returning to their previous practice of Judaism. Throughout the thirteen chapters in Hebrews, the author makes an impassioned plea for the Jewish Christians to remember and be convinced of Jesus' identity as the Messiah, that His promises were assured.

He encouraged them to hold fast to their faith and follow the example of Christ as they endured suffering. I believe the struggle of the Hebrews is like ours. Not in experience—most of us do not face the daily threat of persecution—but their struggle is like ours in perception. I believe the faith of the Hebrews dwindled because they believed a small lie—a lie with far-reaching effects. In his book *Winning the War in Your Mind,* pastor Craig Groeschel says, "A lie believed as truth will affect your life as if it were true."[22] It is often the simple, yet false, perceptions that do the most damage. One of the lies we, and the Hebrews, seem to subconsciously believe is this: *If whatever I'm facing is from God and I am being led by God, then the path will be easy. Maybe not easy, but at least easier than what I am experiencing now.*

When we give our lives to God, pray, go to church, read our Bibles, tithe, etc., we can feel like we have checked all the required boxes of devotion. But when difficult times happen, we are perplexed. We don't understand why God would allow us to experience such pain. We may not voice our questions, but they begin to form in our hearts. Thoughts like: *With all I have done for God, this is what I get for it?* When unexplainable sorrow overwhelms us, we begin to think God isn't holding up His part of the bargain. We think, *This isn't what I signed up for.* However, looking at Scripture and the promises Jesus gives for the Christian life, we read verses that say:

> "In the world you will have tribulation" (John 16:33).

> "Whoever does not bear his own cross and come after me cannot be my disciple" (Luke 14:27).

> "Remember the word that I said to you: 'A servant is not greater than his master.' If they persecuted me, they will also persecute you" (John 15:20).

> In Luke's gospel, Jesus tells the crowds to count the cost of following Him:

> For which of you, desiring to build a tower, does not first sit
> down and count the cost, whether he has enough to complete
> it? Otherwise, when he has laid a foundation and is not able
> to finish, all who see it begin to mock him, saying, "This man
> began to build and was not able to finish." Or what king, going
> out to encounter another king in war, will not sit down first and
> deliberate whether he is able with ten thousand to meet him
> who comes against him with twenty thousand? And if not, while
> the other is yet a great way off, he sends a delegation and asks
> for terms of peace. So therefore, any one of you who does not
> renounce all that he has cannot be my disciple (Luke 14:28–33).

The truth of the Christian life is that it will cost us everything and if this was the end of the story, we should be pitied. However, just as the cross didn't end in death, our journey doesn't end in suffering. Second Corinthians 4:16–17 tells us: "We do not lose heart. Though our outer self is wasting away, our inner self is being renewed day by day. For this light momentary affliction is preparing for us an eternal weight of glory beyond all comparison." Jesus never promises an easy path; quite the opposite. However, He does promise that following God is worth every moment of doubt or affliction. Every ounce of suffering we experience in this world is not meaningless: it produces in us and for us an eternal weight of glory. Therefore, take to heart the passionate call from the author of Hebrews:

> Therefore, since we are surrounded by so great a cloud of
> witnesses, let us also lay aside every weight, and sin which clings
> so closely, and let us run with endurance the race that is set
> before us, looking to Jesus, the founder and perfecter of our
> faith, who for the joy that was set before him endured the cross,
> despising the shame, and is seated at the right hand of the throne
> of God (Heb. 12:1–2).

When I had finished my discovery flight, I walked out of the hangar and tried to get my mind around all I had just experienced. I felt accomplished, but there was also an anger for the perceived danger I felt I was in. Another pilot walked over to me and asked what I felt about my flight. I told him I was a little upset that the instructor would put my life at risk by having me land the plane on my first time in an airplane. I talked about my responsibility to my children and my wife, and I expressed my frustration that the instructor refused to take the controls. Then the pilot said something I didn't expect. I thought he would agree with me, or tell me to grow up, but instead, he chuckled and nodded as he told me, "Paul, there wasn't a moment in that plane when the instructor wasn't in control. You may have felt that it was all on you, but he would not have let that plane crash. His first priority was that you and he got to go home today."

I still don't know if the instructor was exactly wise in the way he handled our flight, but the pilot's words stuck with me. The lie I had believed was that *I* was in control, that everything depended on *my* actions. If that were true, it would have been a harrowing experience, but the pilot was right there ready to take the controls at the first hint of things going south. Pride would have us believe that our hands must always be on the controls. With this belief, it is understandable that we would fear any situation that could possibly extend beyond our control. A lie we believe in our lives as we follow Jesus is that we are in control, that our impact for the kingdom is all in our hands. When we believe this lie, then every heartache is because we weren't faithful enough, every sickness is because we didn't pray enough, and every success is because we worked hard enough or were clever enough. (Remember, the purpose of discipleship is not for us to give great portions of our time and efforts to show what we can offer Jesus; the purpose of our discipleship is to surrender the control of our lives to be used by Jesus.)

We surrender our talents, our abilities, our resources, and even our weaknesses so that a story may be told for the glory of God. If you attempt the Christian journey with a perception that you can work hard enough and be faithful enough to achieve its end, you will end up broken down on the side of the road, blaming God for not giving you a better car. I say this with only love for you: you are not enough for the journey ahead. My saying so may be insulting or infuriating for you, but it is also true. To take a point of illustration from Louie Giglio, I'm not trying to make you feel not enough. I'm hoping to help you see that you are not enough. Though, pride tells us all day and night that we are enough. The daily mantra of our culture could be summed up in the words of Stuart Smalley, a satirical character from Saturday Night Live, who said, "I am good enough, smart enough, and doggone it, people like me!"[23] We live in a culture that regularly affirms and celebrates how we can do anything we set our minds to, but the gospel tells us that we are not enough—which is actually really good news.

The hope of the statement, "You are not enough," is the truth that you were never meant to be enough. It was never a part of God's plan to give you a simple path, one you could take in your own strength. The reason for this, I believe, is two-fold: First, because God wants to do more in you and through you than you are capable of, and second, because God intends to lead you on the journey. You are not alone, you are not in control, and there will be help along the way. Jesus said: "I am the way, and the truth, and the life. No one comes to the Father except through me" (John 14:6). This is not an exclusion; it is an invitation. Jesus knows that only through Him will the path lead to life.

In a world with distractions promising what they cannot deliver and pride saying control will fix everything, Jesus is the way. When you are inundated with false identities and well-intentioned counsels claiming to be wise, Jesus is the truth. When you struggle to know your purpose and potential, Jesus is the life. Jesus wants us to come to the Father, He alone knows the path, and He stands ready to walk it with us.

In a world that says control will fix everything, Jesus is the way.

John 14–16 are three chapters that serve as a farewell discourse that Jesus gave to His disciples. In the last of the three, Jesus said something alarming: "But now I am going to him who sent me" (John 16:5). Put yourself in the position of the disciples. Jesus had told them He was the only way to the Father, then He said, "I'm about to leave." The disciples had grown accustomed to the presence of Jesus. For the past three years, they had gone where He told them to go and had done whatever He told them to do. Now, at the height of His ministry, Jesus would be leaving? How could this be a part of the plan? How could this be good news? But Jesus said His departure was, in fact, good news: "Nevertheless, I tell you the truth: it is to your advantage that I go away, for if I do not go away, the Helper will not come to you. But if I go, I will send him to you" (John 16:7). This is not the first time that Jesus mentioned a helper who was to come.

Back in John 14, Jesus gave the disciples the promise of a helper: "If you love me, you will keep my commandments. And I will ask the Father, and he will give you *another Helper*, to be with you forever" (John 14:15–16, emphasis mine). Who is this helper? The Spirit of truth, or, The Holy Spirit. The question we raised was: how can Jesus leave earth but also lead us on our path? The answer is the Holy Spirit. When Jesus first spoke of the Holy Spirit, He referred to Him as, "another helper." These words are important in understanding not only the blessing of the Holy Spirit but also the nature of God.

The Greek language has two different words for the meaning "another." The first word is, *heteros*, which means, "another of different quality or another kind."[24] This would be like if my son's dog was hit by a car and I bought him a goldfish as a replacement. The second word is, *allos*, which means "another, numerically but of the same kind."[25] This would be like replacing the dead dog with another of the same breed and age. It is an important distinction.

When Jesus said the word, "another," the word used was *allos*. Jesus was saying He would send us a helper equal to Him in both kind and quality. Jesus called the Holy Spirit His equal. In John 10, Jesus said, in talking about His relationship to the Father, "I and the

Father are one" (John 10:30). In these verses we get an understanding that Jesus, the Father, and the Holy Spirit are one—this is where we get the doctrine of the Trinity, which we'll come back to. The second word Jesus used to describe the Holy Spirit was the word "helper." This is the Greek word *parakletos*, which means, "a comforter, helper, advocate, or counselor."[26] So Jesus said He was going away, but then said we would be given a part of God that is one with the Father and Jesus, who will comfort, help, advocate for, and counsel us. Since Jesus, the Father, and the Holy Spirit are one, Jesus was essentially saying what God said to Joshua in the Old Testament: "I will not leave you or forsake you" (Josh. 1:5).

So if Jesus, the Father, and the Holy Spirit are one, why does Jesus say it is better for us that He leaves? There were many times in middle and high school when I longed to see Jesus face-to-face. Mostly, these longings came during times when I was struggling to hang on to my faith. I wanted something concrete I could cling to, something to calm my doubts. If I were to stand with the disciples as Jesus promised, "another Helper," my first thought would probably have been that I would prefer Jesus to stay right where He was. But Jesus, who knows and desires the best for us, said His way was better. The reason is found in the next verses of John 14. "I will ask the Father, and he will give you another Helper, to be with you forever, even the Spirit of truth, whom the world cannot receive, because it neither sees him nor knows him. You know him, for he dwells with you and will be *in you*" (John 14:16–17, emphasis mine).

Remember, the purpose of the gospel is that we would be reconciled to God. When God created the world, Adam and Eve were in direct fellowship with Him. They spoke with Him, walked with Him, and were able to know God personally. When sin entered in, Adam and Eve were removed from the garden, away from the way they had known God. From that point on, the story of Scripture is about God leading us back to a place where we can once again have fellowship with Him. Throughout the Old Testament, God gave the Israelites small imitations of the garden. The first, in the book of Leviticus, was the tabernacle, which housed the ark of the covenant on which God caused His presence to dwell.

In 1 Kings, Solomon built a temple in which the ark would be housed. These imitations created places for God's presence to dwell among His people, yet He was still separated from them. When Jesus took His last breaths on the cross and uttered, "It is finished," everything changed. Matthew tells us, "And behold, the curtain of the temple was torn in two, from top to bottom. And the earth shook, and the rocks were split" (Matt. 27:51). The curtain of the temple was a piece of fabric which served to separate the people from the presence of God. When Jesus took on the sin of the world in death, the barrier between heaven and earth was opened. For the first time since creation, true fellowship with God was once again possible. A new garden was formed: one not found in a tabernacle or maintained by the blood of animals. This new garden resides in the hearts of those who, in faith, put on Jesus and receive the Holy Spirit. It is maintained through the blood of Jesus which is sufficient to cover all sin.

Think about how elated you would be if Jesus stood physically in front of you—the questions you would ask, the stories you would hear, the love you would feel. It would be life-changing. Jesus said that the presence of the Holy Spirit within us is better than if He was physically alongside us for the rest of our lives. That is not to diminish the power of Jesus' physical presence, but to elevate the power of the Holy Spirit's internal presence. Jesus said that the power in Him, the power flowing through everything He did, would be placed inside of us through the Holy Spirit. This is an intimacy with God that Abraham, Moses, Joshua, Samuel, and David never knew. Nebuchadnezzar had counsel in Daniel and God working against him and for him, yet we have so much more. We have the opportunity to be closer to God than any of the heroes of the Old Testament, because we have now been reconciled to God.

The journey to overcoming pride and living out our faith is one on which we need the Holy Spirit. He is our comforter, our helper, our advocate, and our counselor. The path to humility is hard, filled with failure and insecurity. You need a comforter. You cannot successfully navigate this path on your own. You need a helper. Sin will still be a problem and your good deeds will not be enough. You need an advocate. And so often you are going to face circumstances when you will not be able to see any good or purpose. You will have times when you lose sight of who you are in Jesus. You need a counselor to speak encouragement and truth over you. The road ahead is long and difficult. Remember, the presence of the living God resides inside of you. He gives you the purpose and identity you need for the journey. You don't walk alone. There is help along the way.

What did you read that was new to you?

What can you do with this?

How can you pray through this?

Who do you need to talk to about this?

What can this look like in the church?

8

Let Go to Get God

hortly after I became the lead pastor of Lakewood Christian Church, I received a call from a friend who also happens to be named Paul. During the call he asked me how I felt about my new position. I shared my concerns and insecurities about whether I would be able to be what our church needed. Near the end of the call he said, "Paul, I think you need to regularly meet with people who have lived more life than you and who don't necessarily go to Lakewood. I think you need a safe place to share concerns and seek counsel." I told him I thought it was a great idea and the call ended soon after. I genuinely did think it was a wonderful idea, but I didn't really think much more about it after we got off the phone. Two days later, my phone rang again, and it was Paul. "Good news," he told me, "I've got the guys together. I'll see you tomorrow morning in the hospital cafeteria." The next morning, I pulled into the hospital parking lot and began to walk toward the cafeteria, feeling anxious as to what I was walking into.

Today, I still meet with these men almost every week. Mercifully, the time has been pushed back a little, but every Friday, there we are at a table in the cafeteria talking about God, church, concerns, and struggles. Every week we finish by earnestly asking how we can pray for each other and then we pray together. I am eternally grateful for the sanctuary these men have given me. Their wisdom has influenced my leadership and spiritual health more than they know.

One morning, as we were praying at the end of our meeting, I struggled with a thought. In the months leading up to that meeting,

I had become more and more aware of the shocking amount of pride in my heart. It wasn't who I wanted to be. I knew God was moving in our church. I preached with passion, but I felt like a fraud. How dare I preach to these people when the one who needed to hear the messages the most was me? As our group went around the circle praying for each other, I was troubled. *God,* I prayed to myself, *How can I let go of pride? I hate what it does to me. I hate how it creeps into conversations making them more about me. I don't want to be the guy who doesn't listen to people because I'm thinking about what I'm going to say next. I know you don't want this for me, but I don't know how to let go.*

As our prayer finished and we said our goodbyes, in my periphery I saw a hand raised to the air. Looking over, I saw a man at the next table with a smile on his face and his hand in a fist in the air. Something I have learned to greatly love is getting into conversations with complete strangers. Hospitals are easy places to do that. Waving goodbye to my group, I decided I would go over and talk to this man. I had no idea how formative the next thirty minutes of my life would be. In fact, I spent the next two months believing it was possible this man was a real, from heaven to earth, angel. I walked over to the man, whose hand was now down, and introduced myself. "Hi," I said, "my name is Paul." He smiled and said, "Well, that won't be hard to remember, my middle name is Paul, first name is Roy." I shook his hand and said, "I noticed that you had your hand raised in the air while we were praying." His smile got even bigger as he said, "I just love it when the family prays." He then looked me up and down and said, "Looks like you've got a lot to do, it was nice to meet you, but I don't want to keep you." Truthfully, I did have a lot to do. I had been pulled out of my office almost every day that week and the sermon for Sunday was not anywhere close to where I wanted it to be, but I was glued to the spot. "No," I said, "I love talking to people and I've got plenty of time if you would like to talk." He chuckled and said, "Well, then you better grab a seat."

The conversation that followed is hard to describe. It wasn't particularly meaningful in its content. We talked about life, the church, and a few favorite passages of Scripture. I was impressed with his knowledge of the Bible and the authority with which he spoke, but the impactful part of this chance meeting was not the words we spoke, it was the feeling growing inside me. Usually when I meet people in the hospital, I finish our conversations by asking them how I can pray for them, but as this conversation began to wind down, I heard my voice asking a different question: "Roy," I said, "can you pray for me?" Roy's hand, which was surprisingly rough, shot across the table and grabbed mine. With a shaking voice that sounded like I had given him the greatest honor of his life, he asked, "What is it that you want me to say to the Father?" Before I could form a more pastoral response I said, "My pride is killing me and I don't know how to let it go." Tears had started to come to my eyes as Roy sat there silently watching me. As he looked at me, his eyes did not show acceptance, dismissal, or judgment, they looked sad. After a moment, he patted my hand and, with a thick voice, he said, "If you want, I can tell you how to let it go."

This wasn't the response I was expecting, but he had my rapt attention. I nodded assent and he said, "Okay, you let it go by letting it go." I once watched a balloon artist making an elaborate headdress for a child. Putting the final touches on his masterpiece, he twisted one of the balloons, which popped, causing the entire headdress to come apart. His shoulders slumped and he looked dejected. This dejection is the closest I can get to telling you how I felt about his advice. For some reason, I thought I was about to be given the key to a life of freedom from pride, but instead, I was told something I could have easily found in a fortune cookie. My feelings were apparently obvious to Roy who shook his head and said, "You're not getting it." Lost for a response, I said, "No, but I want to."

Still holding my hand in his, he said, "I want to tell you a story. There was a theme park ride that got stuck upside down and in one of the seats there was a little girl who was probably too small to be on it. As the ride hung upside down, the little girl slipped from her harness and wound up hanging from the ride holding on to the handle of her restraint. The girl's father jumped the fence and ran under his daughter. The little girl was crying and screaming, scared to death she was going to fall, but the father yelled up to her, 'Daddy's here, you can let go, I'll catch you.' The girl was too afraid. She yelled out, 'I can't let go, I don't want to fall.' The father shouted again, 'It's the only way baby, you have to let go. Don't worry, I'll catch you.' Again, the little girl screamed, 'I can't, I'm too scared.' The father then shouted up at his beautiful girl, 'Baby, I am your father, I care more about you than my next breath, trust me, let go, I am your father, you will not touch the ground.' The girl then let go of the handle and fell. Her father, true to his word, caught her and carried her back to safety."

A moment of silence passed and then Roy slapped my hand, fairly hard, with his and said, "Paul, you have a Father who loves you so much that He gave His life for you. I know you're scared but let go! He is your Father, and He will not let you hit the ground. Trust Him!" He then gave a curt nod and said, "Now, I'm going to pray." Again, I don't know how to explain this next part well. As Roy prayed over me, I couldn't listen to his prayer. Somehow, his prayer seemed so genuine and intimate that it felt wrong to listen to his words, like I would be eavesdropping on a conversation not meant for me. As Roy prayed, I began to pray. *Father*, I thought, looking for the right words, *whatever this man is praying, please say yes*. At the end of his prayer, Roy slapped my hand once more and said, "Alright, get out of here and go get about your business." I got up and walked out of the hospital without looking back. Once in my car, I broke down. In between sobs, I thanked God earnestly for that moment. The verse that kept coming to my mind was Psalm 8:4, "What is man that you are mindful of him, and the son of man that you care for him?" I prayed, "God, who am I that you would take the time to encourage me? Who am I that you would set up whatever that encounter was?" I left that parking lot very different than when I pulled in.

Letting go of pride is hard. We're not just letting go of certain practices in our lives or ways of thinking. In letting go of pride we are letting go of an idea of ourselves we have spent a lifetime cultivating and curating. To let go of pride you must let go of your entire perceived self, which is a terrifying proposition. Our attachment to pride changes us and develops within us a persona God never intended. The 2001 film *A Beautiful Mind*[27] tells the story of John Nash, a brilliant mathematician and future Nobel Prize winner, who suffers from paranoid schizophrenia.

In letting go of pride we are letting go of who we think we are.

In the film, John experiences real relationships with people who turn out to be delusions. Near the end, John has a final conversation with one of his delusions whom he had believed to be his roommate at Princeton University. The interesting thing about the scene is that, while John knows the person he is talking to is not real, he still has affection for him and has difficulty letting him go. There is a fascinating tension within this story between John's hatred of his illness and his love for some of his delusions. In the same way, we can feel a hatred for pride in our lives and yet still feel affection for the persona it has created in us.

We feel affection because the persona is what we know, it is what we have known, and it is where we find comfort. We like the version of ourselves that is puffed up, who has it all figured out and can do no wrong. In the film John eventually concludes that to hold on to his delusions would be to embrace and even revel in his sickness. Although the delusions bring him comfort, they are ultimately a product of the sickness of his mind, and he decides he would rather be healthy than remain in the comfort of his delusions. While the persona of pride can bring comfort in a known, though false, identity, we must come to the point where we desire our God-given identity over the fabricated persona of pride. In letting go of pride, you let go of the sickness you hate and of the persona you may have come to love.

For Nebuchadnezzar to arrive at the place he ended up required a drastic event, one that he was not prepared to take on his own. He had built a personal identity that could not be dependent on anyone but himself. Therefore, for Nebuchadnezzar to be able to discover who he really was in the grand scheme, the entirety of who he was would have to be rewritten. It is for this reason that letting go of pride is both a difficult and fearful choice.

In a collection of journal entries by missionary Jim Elliot, he wrote a now famous phrase: "He is no fool who gives what he cannot keep to gain that which he cannot lose."[28] The apostle Paul wrote a similar statement in his letter to the church in Philippi, "For to me to live is Christ, and to die is gain" (Phil. 1:21). When we follow God, our question should not be, what will we lose, but rather, what will we gain? The currency pride offers can only buy the trinkets of a worldly market, little toys that offer a moment of satisfaction but are soon broken or found unfulfilling. Whether it be position or possessions, pride offers a promise of fulfillment that it cannot fulfill. The words of Jim Elliot and the apostle Paul speak of a greater and true wealth that supersedes all the pursuits of this world in both value and longevity. In speaking about the kingdom of heaven, Jesus told this parable: "The kingdom of heaven is like treasure hidden in a field, which a man found and covered up. Then in his joy he goes and sells all that he has and buys that field" (Matt. 13:44).

Imagine finding something of such value that you sell all your possessions to obtain it. Think about going through your house and selling, not just your big-ticket items, but even the simple, sentimental ones. There may be a momentary feeling of loss as you part with these, but that loss is made not only bearable but joyful because you know what you are about to gain. The kingdom of heaven is so precious in value and desirable to be obtained that anything we give up or release in its pursuit is not worth comparing to the joy we will experience once we have it.

I am not making light of the fears or struggles that come with letting go of pride. I am saying that the joy of the kingdom of heaven is such that any loss will not matter in comparison. This is the promise we have from Jesus and so, I repeat to you the words told to me by a stranger in a hospital cafeteria: "You have a Father who loves you so much that He gave His life for you. I know you're scared but let go! He is your Father, and He will not let you hit the ground. Trust Him!" This is the key to freedom and joy. It is the answer to the question fueling your desires and decisions without you even knowing it. This is the open gate to the life you have been pursuing, even if by the wrong paths. Let go so you may gain what God has for you and so you might discover who you really are.

What did you read that was new to you?

What can you do with this?

How can you pray through this?

Who do you need to talk to about this?

What can this look like in the church?

9

The Fear of the Fall

The prospect of letting go and trusting God is attractive, but its application is tricky. When we look at the results of Nebuchadnezzar's humility, we may desire to be in the same place of acknowledgment and submission to God's will that he was. Still, when we look at the entirety of Nebuchadnezzar's story, when we see the humiliation and failure that he went through, it is enough to bring our ambition to a screeching halt. Proverbs rightly tells us that pride comes before the fall, but does this mean that there is an impending fall in the pursuit of genuine humility? We can genuinely desire humility, but we also can be equally genuine in our fear of the fall. In our fight against pride, we must address and answer the question: does genuine humility require a devastating fall?

In the first chapter, we defined pride as elevating ourselves to a position that rightfully and solely belongs to God. Let's think about this from the perspective of Mt. Sinai in the nineteenth chapter of Exodus. God had led the Israelites out of slavery to the Egyptians in spectacular fashion using plagues, tornadic pillars of fire, and even parting the waters of an entire sea so that His people could cross on dry ground! He then led them to the foot of Mt. Sinai on which He caused His glory to settle and charged the people not to touch the mountain. Essentially, He said that the mountain belonged to Him and His holiness. Therefore, to step onto the mountain would be to place yourself in a position that solely belonged to God. This is a physical illustration of our spiritual struggle with pride. When our steps are directed by pride, it leads us to places and positions that belong only to God. And so, with pride as a guide, we find ourselves on trails that slowly and consistently climb the mountain of God; each step bringing us higher and higher into places that are not meant for us. Moreover, the longer we stay on this path, the higher we rise and the farther the inevitable fall will be. It is understandable, then, to feel a sense of foreboding fear when we realize our position: that we are now standing at the lookout of a mountain we should never have climbed facing a fall we fear we may not survive.

In one of the more trying seasons of ministry we have faced, my wife and I spent three days of intentional prayer and reflection at Glen Eyrie Castle in Colorado Springs. During one of the afternoons, we decided it would be best to take some time to seek God on our own. In an act of extreme self-unawareness and hubris, I decided that I would connect best to God by taking on the hardest trail the property had to offer. The trail started easily enough as a lookout trail that would eventually branch off into the more difficult loop. As I walked, I began to pray an impassioned prayer asking God why He had brought us to this point, whether I was meant for ministry at all, and begging Him for a sign. Ironically, while I prayed this prayer for a sign, I completely missed the sign that would have taken me on the loop trail. Twenty minutes later, I unknowingly arrived at the lookout. I even remembered thinking, "Man, they should have called this the lookout, it is beautiful!" Thinking I was still on the loop trail I continued my quest by stepping off onto what I later discovered was a wildlife path. I only made it ten feet before the trail disintegrated under my feet, leaving me to fall and slide down about fifty feet of loose shale. I managed to stop my descent by grabbing onto a tree, but this left me in a precarious situation. Each time I attempted to climb back up to the trail, I would end up sliding farther down the shale, which wouldn't have concerned me too much except that, about one hundred feet down from where I was, the shale slide abruptly ended in a sheer drop into a boulder valley. So, there I was, quite literally between a rock and a hard place. I knew that I needed to get back on the path, but I was paralyzed from the fear that any action I could take would end in a fall. Reaching the point of exhaustion, I finally came to accept that the path upward which I had previously identified as safe, was now closed to me. To get down, I would have to find a less conventional and possibly more dangerous way. Looking down, past the cliff and the boulder valley, I saw another trail that my wife and I had taken the previous day: a path that I knew was safe, solid, and flat. Giving up my efforts to go upward, I began to work slowly sideways and downward until I reached the top of a boulder at the edge of the drop. What followed were three hours in which I slowly and carefully eased my way down between boulders until I finally reached the level ground of the safe trail. Ironically, I chose the original trail in hopes of having a strenuous hike filled with meaningful prayer and the path I ended up taking was one on which I experienced some of the most genuine and urgently meaningful prayers of that whole weekend!

I went on that hike with a plan. When the plan went south, I eventually became paralyzed by the fear of a potential fall while I desperately tried to get back to the place where my plan failed, not realizing that the previous path was one on which I was never supposed to be. To get down to safety then required that a new path be forged. When you find yourself on the mountain of God, you will not be able to descend on the paths that brought you there.

When God guides us from the mountain of pride, He will not choose paths that we would automatically identify as logical and safe, nor will He take us on the paths that got us into this position; He will guide us down precarious ways on which we will have to completely trust in Him. The way down the mountain is slow and intentional. Not following our intentions and directions, but God's. Coming down the mountain of pride is much like coming off any physical mountain in the world. There are generally two ways down: one, a slow and deliberate descent, or two, a much faster and more devastating fall. Nebuchadnezzar fell off the mountain face-first and landed in a pile of dung at its base. Reading his story, it seems that falling was the inevitable outcome of his pride, but does that have to be your story? The short answer is no, but even if the fall is unavoidable, the destination of humility is worth the price. However, you have several things working for your benefit that Nebuchadnezzar did not.

First, you have the church. Nebuchadnezzar lived in a culture that praised his actions and enforced all the ideals that built his pride. Today, we have a culture that does much the same. The pursuit of happiness has been so deeply enshrined in the hearts of people that it has become the primary focus of life. When happiness, which is circumstantial and fleeting, becomes the ultimate goal of life, the culture will then encourage and reinforce all self-proclaimed identities and pursuits that lead to it. However, in the church, when we surround ourselves with faithful friends who love us too much to enforce false identities, who, in love, prioritize our eternity over our moment by calling out our pride, when we surround ourselves with a genuine community of faith, we will not be able to walk up the mountain of pride without the hands of beloved brothers and sisters in Christ around our ankles, willing us to stop. Not only do they impede our travel up the mountain, but they also help facilitate our descent. Pride is a universal struggle, which means, as you make your way down the mountain of pride to the valley of humility, you will have encouragement, mentorship, and hands to pull you back up when you stumble because they are taking the journey with you. You don't have to suffer the same pitfalls as your brothers and sisters because, in greater wisdom, you are able to learn from their mistakes. In this way you lean on those who are ahead of you and lead those behind you as we all walk off this mountain together.

Second, as we discussed in Chapter 7, you have the Holy Spirit of the living God dwelling within you. Paul tells us in Galatians, "Walk by the Spirit, and you will not gratify the desires of the flesh" (Gal. 5:16). He goes on to say in verse twenty-five, "If we live by the Spirit, let us also keep in step with the Spirit" (Gal. 5:25). Our steps come from the Holy Spirit. He speaks directly to our hearts and indirectly through others in whom He also dwells. You have the Holy Spirit as a guide in your life walking before you, showing you the places where you can safely place your feet. Psalm 23 speaks of God as a shepherd who leads His sheep in paths of righteousness. For the sheep to get safely down the path, they must pay attention to the shepherd, stepping only where he steps because the shepherd not only knows the way, but he also knows the dangers of the journey. The Holy Spirit is our guide; He directs us past pitfalls, reminds us of our destination, and encourages us to remain faithful and to place our trust in Him. For the destination to be reached, the sheep must trust the shepherd. To trust the shepherd is to allow the shepherd to lead. The sheep do not get to pick the path, they follow the shepherd. Pride tells us that we know the best paths and which dangers to avoid. Pride insists that control of the journey is best left in our hands. The Holy Spirit gently and consistently reminds us that this undertaking is too big for our hands, as He opens His to take the burden from our shoulders.

Third, you have Jesus, who could have come to this world, lived in a palace, overthrown Rome, and led His people and the world better than any king ever had or ever would, but He did not do that. Jesus did not choose a palace, He chose a stable; He did not choose prestige, He chose humility. Jesus made Himself into a humble servant, which was then taken to extreme lengths as He was publicly humiliated, stripped naked, beaten, ridiculed, and killed by those who were not worthy even to be in His presence. An outside observer would look at the sum of Jesus' life and declare it a waste. And it is easy to come to that conclusion, especially when we think of what could have been possible if Jesus had come as a ruler. His intentional choice then to come as a servant shows us that He was aiming to accomplish more than simply turning the Israelites into the greatest kingdom on earth. He did come to vanquish an enemy, but His target was one far greater and more savage than Rome. Jesus came to deal a lethal and lasting blow to sin and death by claiming the dominion of the earth back from the hands of Satan. This goal could not be conquered by armies or influence, it could only be accomplished through sacrifice. Therefore, in Jesus' sacrifice we find that our struggle against pride is a battle that has already been fought and won. Second Corinthians says, "For our sake he made him to be sin who knew no sin, so that in him we might become the righteousness of God" (2 Cor. 5:21). Jesus has taken the fall for you. So, whether you come off the mountain of pride a step at a time or as a result of a great and devastating fall, you will not land in the condemnation that is the natural and just destination of pride; you will land in the arms of a loving savior who bears the scars of the fall you rightly should have taken.

Jesus doesn't ask that we pay Him back for His gracious mercy, as if we could repay even the smallest amount of what we owe Him; He simply gives the invitation to follow Him. Much like He did with each of His disciples, Jesus gives the invitation now to you. You are not now nor will you ever be worthy of this invitation, but Jesus doesn't call people based on worth. When He walked the earth, He called fishermen, tax collectors, and zealots to be His followers. None of them brought sufficient talent, obedience, courage, or any number of potential benefits to the table, yet Jesus called them to be His followers all the same. However, in teaching His disciples what it would require to follow Him, Jesus did say, "If anyone would come after me, let him deny himself and take up his cross daily and follow me" (Luke 9:23).

Genuine humility absolutely requires a fall; it may not require a devastating one, but it does require a daily one. If we are to follow Jesus, each day we must acknowledge Jesus' place above us. He is the guide and decider of our steps. He is the one who picks our priorities and destinations because He is the one who sees the larger picture of the grander journey in which we are completely insignificant. That may not hit you well, but the fact that Jesus chooses us insignificant people to accomplish His work gives us an incredible and unfathomable significance. Look at the people that Jesus chose in the Gospels. Without Him, they would have led a regular first-century life with no consequences. However, through Jesus, their lives became greater than their individual stories. They spoke boldly, led faithfully, stumbled, and stood, eventually giving their lives to this greater mission. And the glory they found was of such quantity and quality that it was not worth comparing to the temporary suffering and loss they experienced in this world. In Jesus we have a wonderfully insignificant significance, the complete impact of which we will not grasp until we stand with Him in His eternal kingdom. Pride desires to rob us of any lasting significance by offering a brief façade of honor and praise in this world. We need to come off the mountain. There will be a time when we will stand with God at the summit of His kingdom, but our place and purpose in this world is found in the valley. Therefore, how we get off the mountain is not nearly as important as that we get off the mountain.

Perhaps the fall is not something to be feared but sought. Perhaps it is not a punishment of God, but a gift from God so that we can finally see this life from the perspective of the eternal. We should long for the humility and purpose of the valley. It is not easy to contemplate the cost of sincerely following Jesus, but the end result is worth the struggle. To step onto this path then, you must come to the point of submission where you earnestly and perhaps fearfully say to God, "If you can't guide me down the mountain, kick me off, because I want to be in genuine relationship more than I want to be in control." You are surrounded by the church, the Holy Spirit, the angels of heaven, and Jesus Himself, willing you to discover the gift of the fall and the purpose of the valley. Let go, for it is only in letting go that we discover who we truly are.

> *Perhaps the fall is not something to be feared but sought.*

What did you read that was new to you?

What can you do with this?

How can you pray through this?

Who do you need to talk to about this?

What can this look like in the church?

10

Remember
Who You Are

When I was fourteen my grandmother gave me a lame gift. I have a feeling that, as I talk about this gift, some of you will no longer be on my side. In the days before ancestry.com, my grandmother spent years compiling a complete family history. She interviewed family members, searched her way through libraries of genealogies, and typed out many of her own recollections. The result of this labor of love was a document of more than three hundred pages which detailed our lineage going back to the eighteenth century. This gift was thoughtful, thorough, and completely unappreciated by me, a high schooler who would have rather been given money or a pager. Now, looking back on all my birthdays and Christmases, I don't remember the money I received or even the toys. I never did get that pager—but in hindsight, I do not think I missed out on that technological revolution. I don't remember any of the gifts given to me by my grandparents, but I do cherish those three hundred pages my grandmother poured so much time and care into. When I finally sat down and read the contents of that notebook, I was captivated by the stories of the Vanderveers who had come before me. I was able to see in its pages the moment God became a core part of our family's beliefs, and the pastors, missionaries, and kingdom workers who came as a result. Even today, I sit with my children and flip through its pages telling them of the legacy they have been given. This is a gift no human will ever be able to top.

At the beginning of the document, there's a page showing the Vanderveer coat of arms. Each part of the coat of arms has meaning, but at the bottom there is a phrase in Latin: "Aut Inveniam Aut Faciam," which means, "What we undertake, we do." This saying was repeated to me in varying ways throughout my childhood. I remember once when my grandfather caught me trying to take a shortcut on yardwork, he said, "Do you really want to be known as someone who accepts a job and does it poorly? You said you would do this; a lot rides on you doing it well. Remember who you are." This conversation had very little to do with the yard. As he told me years later, I had been given a legacy from those who came before me, and my grandfather's hope was that this legacy would continue in me and beyond me into future generations.

So who are you?

Scripture tells us we are created in God's image (Gen. 1:26), we are chosen (Eph. 1:4), we are justified and redeemed (Rom. 3:24), we are adopted (Rom. 8:15), we are God's children (John 1:12), we are heirs of His kingdom (Rom. 8:17), we are forgiven (Eph. 1:7), we are new (2 Cor. 5:17), and we are loved (John 3:16; Rom. 5:8). This is who we are. When we forget who we are, pride prevails and sin enters in.

One of the great heroes of the Bible, in fact, the only man to be called a man after God's own heart, is David. David was the picture of humility and devotion. As a shepherd he wrote songs about God's majesty and enduring love. When David came face-to-face with a giant on a battlefield, he responded to the man's taunting not with self-aggrandizing bravado but by telling the warrior that God would strike him down and win the victory. When David was being hunted by Saul, David's respect and submission to the will of God was so absolute that he put his own life in jeopardy rather than going against God's plans—even though he had already been anointed to be the king of Israel. What an incredible picture David is of what it is like to follow God in different seasons and through the obstacles of life. However, apart from being known for his devotion, David is also known for his great sin.

Second Samuel 1 tells the story of King David, who while walking on his roof one afternoon, saw a woman taking a bath. He lingered and gawked at her beauty, for she was very beautiful. Sending for his servants, David asked about her and was told she was Bathsheba, the wife of one of his finest warriors, Uriah. Knowing David's past heart of humility and devotion, it would be natural to think that, at this point, David would have put her out of his mind while silently congratulating Uriah on marrying such a beautiful woman, but that is not what he did. Instead, David sent messengers to Bathsheba, brought her to the palace, took her to bed, and sent her on her way. If the story ended there, it would be enough to conclude that David had compromised his character, but it was only the beginning of his depravity.

After a time, David found out that Bathsheba had become pregnant. To spare his reputation, David quickly sent word for Uriah to come back from battle under the guise of giving him a report. David hoped Uriah would come back, give his report, and go to bed with his wife before returning to the front. This plan, if successful, would have allowed David's indiscretions to remain secret while also keeping his reputation intact, but such was not to be.

Upon giving a report to the king, Uriah was encouraged to go home and see his wife. David even doubled down by sending along gifts from the king. However, Uriah didn't go home, he walked to the door of the king's house and slept next to the servants. When David found out, he directly urged Uriah to go and be with his wife to which Uriah responded: "The ark and Israel and Judah dwell in booths, and my lord Joab and the servants of my lord are camping in the open field. Shall I then go to my house, to eat and to drink and to lie with my wife? As you live, and as your soul lives, I will not do this thing" (2 Sam. 11:11). Oh what a tragedy that, only a short time before, David would have loved and honored Uriah's character, but faced with his impending humiliation, David came up with a new plan. He once again invited Uriah into his presence, giving him much to drink. Then, with Uriah drunk, David thought that surely then Uriah would go to be with his wife. But Uriah once more slept with the servants. Seemingly out of options, David did the unthinkable. The next morning David wrote a letter to the commander of his armies with orders to place Uriah on the front lines and, when the fighting was severe, for the army to pull back from Uriah so he would be killed. David then took this death warrant and placed it in Uriah's hands, trusting in Uriah's honor that he would not read the words. After this, David remained in his palace to wait for word of Uriah's death.

How can someone so humble, so devoted to God, do such a thing? Surely this couldn't be the same David we read about in earlier chapters. What happened? The answer to these questions is tragic and simple. At the beginning of 2 Samuel 11, we're told the reason. "In the spring of the year, the time when kings go out to battle, David sent Joab, and his servants with him, and all Israel. And they ravaged the Ammonites and besieged Rabbah. But David remained at Jerusalem" (2 Sam. 11:1). In the springtime, *when kings go to war*, David, the king, was in Jerusalem. The wording of this verse intentionally shows the source of David's failure. David was the king, but instead of leading his men, he stayed home.

How ironic that both Nebuchadnezzar and David came to the summit of their pride while standing on rooftops gazing at their kingdoms. As any DIY Christmas lighter will tell you, rooftops are dangerous places that can lead to devastating falls. For Nebuchadnezzar and David, however, their rooftop was not just a physical roof, but a spiritual summit of pride where they could gaze at the accomplishments, which they had allowed to give their lives meaning. We are not immune to these rooftops. While we may never stand and look out on a literal kingdom of palaces and cities, our kingdoms are no less imitations of those that ensnared the affections of the Old

Testament kings. When we look out at our accomplishments, possessions, and social standing, we are easily tempted to ascribe these as products of our own efforts and willpower. The prophet Isaiah in speaking about righteousness said, "We have all become like one who is unclean, and all our righteous deeds are like a polluted garment. We all fade like a leaf, and our iniquities, like the wind, take us away" (Isa. 64:6). This does not mean that our righteous deeds have no value, but when our efforts remain in our own hands for our glory, they become worthless things that are only good to be thrown out with the trash. The value of any good that we do in this life is found when we take our righteousness and place it in the hands of the one to whom all righteousness belongs. In the Gospel of Luke, Jesus says, "So you also, when you have done all that you were commanded, say, 'We are unworthy servants; we have only done what was our duty'" (Luke 17:10). Everything we are is found in Jesus. He alone can take our good deeds and escalate them to have an impact that is far beyond their intrinsic value. The rooftops of our lives belong to God; He is the one who builds the kingdoms of man, but when we place ourselves on the gables, we not only assume a responsibility and role that is not our own, but we also forget who we are in the process.

Standing on both a physical and spiritual rooftop, David forgot who he was. He had become so entrenched in his own glory as the king he forgot why his position even existed. This is evident not only in his staying in Jerusalem but also in the way he pursued Bathsheba. On his roof David saw something he wanted. He then reasoned that since he was the king and since he had the power to do so, he should get what he wanted. He may have even justified that the stresses of leadership afforded him indulgences. In the pride of his position, David took what was not his to take. David knew his name and his position but had forgotten his calling and identity.

Pride is a thief of our identity, making us think we know who we are by touting our accomplishments or talents, our position or power, and our good qualities. Yet at the same time, pride is falsely propping our sense of self up, leading us closer and closer to God's gracious humbling in our lives. Forgetting who we are will lead us straight into the arms of sin.

Pride is a thief of our identity, making us think we know ourselves.

In the effort to build up our feelings of self-worth, we create statues of ourselves depicting who we think we are. Nebuchadnezzar literally did this in Daniel 3. However, these statues have brittle feet and will topple at the smallest change in circumstance, leaving us to wonder who we are and what we do now. Pride steals an identity set in stone and replaces it with one made of paper. Remember how I defined pride? It is the elevating of ourselves to a position that rightfully belongs to God. Humility then, is when we know God alone is sovereign, that He alone tells us who we are.

In the Gospel of Luke, Jesus gave a helpful illustration. Speaking to a group of invited guests at a Pharisee's house, Jesus said:

> When you are invited by someone to a wedding feast, do not sit down in a place of honor, lest someone more distinguished than you be invited by him, and he who invited you both will come and say to you, "Give your place to this person," and then you will begin with shame to take the lowest place. But when you are invited, go and sit in the lowest place, so that when your host comes he may say to you, "Friend, move up higher." Then you will be honored in the presence of all who sit at the table with you. For everyone who exalts himself will be humbled, and he who humbles himself will be exalted" (Luke 14:8–11).

If we look at this passage as speaking of two different people, we see that, at the end of the story, only one of the guests knows where they belong at the table. Pride urges us to stake out our place to ensure our position, but in humility, not only are we honored but we also find out exactly where we belong. In the same way, pride blinds us to who we really are and where we are meant to be, while humility allows Jesus not only to honor us but to show us exactly where we fit at His table. Therefore, humility is not the loss of self; it is the discovery of who we are and where we fit—it is the fastest and straightest path to security and self-knowledge.

My aunt, Gena, has experienced periods of loss and heartache in her life. She once told me of a night when, in her house, she fell to her knees in prayer and tears. Her prayer was honest and simple. "God," she said, "I just need to know what you think of me." In this prayer, Gena laid out her greatest fear and insecurity—that God's thoughts of her might mirror her own. She felt defeated and worthless, and she was worried God might agree. How much would you give to know, really know, what God thinks when He thinks of you? Would you approach this question with fear of what it might reveal? In *The Meaning of Marriage*, Tim Keller writes, "The gospel is this: We are more sinful and flawed in ourselves than we ever dared believe, yet at the very same time we are more loved and accepted in Jesus Christ than we ever dared hope."[29] In another work Keller says, "The gospel is that I am so sinful that Jesus had to die for me, yet so loved and valued that Jesus was glad to die for me. This leads to deep humility and deep confidence at the same time. I can't feel superior to anyone, and yet I have nothing to prove to anyone."[30] The truth is that God loves you so much He would rather die than spend eternity without you. This was His plan from the beginning, and He has and will see it through to the end, not because we add anything to Him, but because He loves us and wants us.

God doesn't want your contributions; He simply wants you. The creator and sustainer of the universe wants you. He wants to tell you who you really are and reveal your great and fulfilling purpose. He doesn't want to watch you walk down dead-end paths toward a self-prescribed definition of success. He wants to open heaven and reveal the wonders of what He had in mind when He created you. He wants you to experience the deep satisfaction of being who you really are and doing what you were created to do. He wants to give you

Himself, and humility is the only way God can give you Himself. He is simply too big to share the throne of your heart with your ego.

When Daniel interpreted Nebuchadnezzar's dream, he finished with this advice, "Therefore, O king, let my counsel be acceptable to you: break off your sins" (Dan. 4:27). Daniel's advice to the king was to break off and renounce his sins. In the battle against pride, one of the hardest steps is letting go of the hand of pride. The Spirit of God who dwells within us can point out our pride and lead us toward humility, but too often, when we come to the strongholds of pride in our lives, we just can't let them go because we have attached so much of our identity to them. If we are going to root out our pride from our lives, we must resolve to let it fall away so humility can take its place. This is a long-fought process, but at its core, the fuel for the fight comes from an understanding that you are not fighting for an identity you hope to one day possess; you are fighting to reclaim who you have been from the beginning. God created you as a bearer of His image. Through the death, resurrection, and ascension of Jesus, you have been given an intercessor and advocate as you pursue this incredible life which slowly and consistently brings you back to your true self. You are the child of the Great King. Pride would have you settle for less than you are. Remember who you are and refuse to settle for the lesser pursuits of this world.

What did you read that was new to you?

What can you do with this?

How can you pray through this?

Who do you need to talk to about this?

What can this look like in the church?

Take the First Step

One of the most difficult things when starting something new is taking the first step. The first time I ever walked into a gym, I looked at the different machines and weights with no idea how to use them. I saw people who were much farther along in their journey and felt intimidated, as if I didn't really belong. I also saw a few people who I felt a little farther along than, which gave me hope in a, *Well, if they can do it*, kind of way. I felt all these things without even venturing into the locker rooms. What I later discovered was that most of the people in the gym were going after the same things and enjoyed encouraging others on the same path.

It is intimidating to start the process of addressing and overcoming pride. It requires sacrifice and brings so many insecurities to light. As you step on this road, you will see some who are well ahead of you, as well as those who are struggling along behind you. In the family of faith, though, we walk together. We encourage those behind us and learn from those ahead as we all walk toward the same destination.

I implore you, take the first step. The fear of the path can keep you from beginning the journey. Once you begin, you will see you are not alone in your struggles and that your insecurities are shared by your travel companions; this is the beauty of the church. We are not a group of saints who have figured it out but a collection of faulty followers who are trying to figure it out together.

The word "stir" is a curious addition to the verse in Hebrews 10 which reads, "Let us consider how to stir up one another to love and good works, not neglecting to meet together, as is the habit of some, but encouraging one another, and all the more as you see the Day drawing near" (Heb. 10:24–25). This is the Greek word *paroxusmos*.[31] I had often believed this word to be more closely related to the idea of encouraging one another toward good works, but the meaning of this word is one that, in most contexts, would seem to be more negative in its application. When translated, *paroxusmos* means to incite, provoke, or irritate. Therefore, a more literal translation of this verse would be to say, "Consider how to incite and irritate each other to love and good works." If the church is merely a weekend obligation and event we go to, this verse is controversial in its application. However, if the church is a family, this verse is only logical.

So often within families, between husbands and wives or parents and children, failures are called out and corrected. When this happens, it is irritating for the purpose of provoking right action and well-being. Dietrich Bonhoeffer said in his book *Life Together*, "Nothing is so cruel as the tenderness that consigns another to his sin. Nothing could be more compassionate than the severe rebuke that calls a brother back from his sin."[32]

In my life, I have had great friends point out the actions or attitudes of mine not aligned with my faith and calling. These conversations were awkward, irritating, and necessary, because true familial responsibility requires us to say, "I love you too much to let you go down this path without saying a word of rebuke." As you contemplate stepping out onto the road to begin the journey of transformation, find people to walk with you who will not silently watch you fall but will pull you back from the edge. Surround yourself with a family of faith and allow yourself to be vulnerable with them. Together, breathe the air of heaven in worship, prayer, and study; share stories of the provision and forgiveness of God and remind each other often of your identity as beloved children of God. You were never meant to take this journey alone, and you don't have to. You have a shepherd who guides you, the Holy Spirit within you, and the church to surround you. Even if your first steps are as awkward as a newborn deer's, take the steps anyway. They will be the first of many and will transform you as you discover the life you were created for.

In Matthew 28, Jesus gives a final commission to the church. As He concludes He says, "And behold, I am with you always, to the end of the age" (Matt. 28:20). You have a savior who will never leave your side. He will protect, guide, and provide for you as you are daily transformed to be more like Him until you enter the reward and rest of His eternal kingdom. In the meantime, pick up your cross and step onto the road. There is no telling where you will be swept off to. As you now put down this book and hopefully take that first fearful step in your journey, let us finish with the words of Paul to the church in Thessalonica: "Now may the God of peace himself sanctify you completely, and may your whole spirit and soul and body be kept blameless at the coming of our Lord Jesus Christ. He who calls you is faithful; he will surely do it" (1 Thess. 5:23–24).

My prayers are for you. Be blessed in the journey.

What's Next?

By far the most effective way to grow in your spiritual maturity is consistent time reading and studying Scripture. The following verses are intended to whet your appetite and act as a springboard for further study in the deep well of scripture. As a further resource, a guide for effective bible study methods can be found at: lakewoodnext.com/biblestudymethods.

Pride:

Proverbs 16:18–19
Jeremiah 9:23–24
Matthew 23:12
Luke 18:9–14
Romans 12:16
James 4:6–7

Humility:

Psalm 131:1
Isaiah 53:7–8
Isaiah 57:15
Micah 6:8
Matthew 11:29
Matthew 18:4
Luke 14:11
Philippians 2:3–11
James 4:10

Identity:

Romans 8:17
Romans 8:37
2 Corinthians 5:17
Ephesians 2:10
Ephesians 5:8–17
1 Peter 2:9
1 John 3:1

The Holy Spirit:

Ezekiel 36:26–28
John 14:16–17
John 14:26
John 15:26–16:15
Acts 2:1–4
Romans 8:26
Galatians 5:22–23
1 Corinthians 12:13
2 Corinthians 3:17

Further Resources

Pride and Humility

- Mere Christianity – C. S. Lewis
- Humility – Andrew Murray
- The Freedom of Self Forgetfulness – Timothy Keller

The Holy Spirit

- The Forgotten God – Francis Chan
- The Familiar Stranger – Tyler Staton

Christian Life

- The Ruthless Elimination of Hurry – John Mark Comer
- Practicing the Way – John Mark Comer
- Winning the War in Your Mind – Craig Groeschel
- Renovation of the Heart – Dallas Willard
- Living in Christ's Presence – Dallas Willard

Prayer

- Praying Like Monks, Living Like Fools – Tyler Staton
- Prayer: Experiencing Awe and Intimacy with God – Timothy Keller
- Prayer: Finding the Heart's True Home – Richard Foster

NEXT
RESOURCE

The goal of Lakewood:Next is to provide a next step for all who are seeking to grow in their relationship and devotion to Jesus regardless of where they are in their discipleship journey. Please visit our website, lakewoodnext.com, to find a growing collection of books, video teachings, articles, and daily video devotions designed to help you in your journey. Whether you are looking to deepen your understanding, find encouragement, or connect with a community of believers, our website has something for you.

Notes

1. H1347b

2. C. S. Lewis, *Mere Christianity* (London: William Collins, 2012), 122.

3. Lewis, *Mere Christianity*, 123.

4. Lewis, *Mere Christianity*, 196–197.

5. Louie Giglio, "Louie Giglio Our God Is Indescribable," *iUniteinChrist*, April 11, 2022, YouTube, 7:54, youtube.com/watch?v=aVsqCLyoU3o.

6. H3046

7. Timothy Keller, *Galatians for You* (The Good Book Company, 2013), 180.

8. Mike Donehey, "Why I Stopped Asking God to Use Me," *Outreach Magazine*, August 13, 2019, outreachmagazine.com/resources/books/christian-living-books/45591-why-i-stopped-asking-god-to-use-me.html.

9. Rick Atchley, "Revelation by Rick Atchley," *The Hills Church*, SoundCloud, 34:39, soundcloud.com/thehillschurch/sets/revelation-by-rick-atchley.

10. Timothy Keller, *Prayer: Experiencing Awe and Intimacy with God* (New York: Penguin Books, 2014), 48.

11. Keller, *Prayer*, 80.

12. Examples of the Israelites being admonished for forgetting God: Judges 3:7; 1 Samuel 12:9; Isaiah 17:10; 51:13; Jeremiah 2:32; 3:21; 13:25; 18:15; 23:27; Ezekiel 22:12; 23:25; Hosea 2:13; 4:6; 8:14; 13:6.

13. C. S. Lewis, *The Four Loves* (London: William Collins, 2016), 74.

14. Timothy Keller, *The Meaning of Marriage: Facing the Complexities of Commitment with the Wisdom of God* (New York: Penguin Books, 2011), 101.

15. J. R. R. Tolkien, *The Lord of the Rings: The Fellowship of the Rings* (New York: Ballentine Books, 1980), 110.

16. G3340

17. G3326

18. G3539

19. Samuel Chand, *Leadership Pain: The Classroom for Growth* (Nashville: Thomas Nelson, 2015), 15.

20. *Alcoholics Anonymous Big Book 4th ed.* (New York: Alcoholics Anonymous World Services, 2002), 85.

21. C. S. Lewis, *The Last Battle* (New York: Harper Collins, 1956), 211.

22. Craig Groeschel, *Winning the War in Your Mind* (Grand Rapids: Zondervan Books, 2021), 12.

23. Saturday Night Live, 1992

24. G2087

25. G243

26. G3875

27. *A Beautiful Mind*, directed by Ron Howard (Hollywood: Universal Studios, 2001).

28. Jim Elliot, *The Journals of Jim Elliot: Missionary, Martyr, Man of God*, ed. Elisabeth Elliot (Grand Rapids: Revell, 2020), 174.

29. Keller, *The Meaning of Marriage*, 44.

30. Timothy Keller, *The Reason for God* (New York: Penguin Books, 2008), 181.

31. G3948

32. Dietrich Bonhoeffer, *Life Together* (New York: Harper and Row, 1954), 107.

About the Author

PAUL VANDERVEER was raised in Muskogee, Oklahoma. In 2010 he graduated from Ozark Christian College with a Bachelor of Christian Ministry. Following graduation, Paul worked in student ministry until becoming the lead pastor at Lakewood Christian Church in September 2019 where he continues to serve today. Paul lives in McAlester, Oklahoma, with his wife, Mallory, and their five children.

www.ingramcontent.com/pod-product-compliance
Lightning Source LLC
Chambersburg PA
CBHW022009100426
42736CB00041B/1174